Resources
for
Renewal

George E. Worrell
Editor

Broadman Press NASHVILLE, TENNESSEE

Dewey Decimal Classification: 262
Subject Heading: CHURCH RENEWAL

Library of Congress Catalog Card Number: 75-8375
Printed in the United States of America

Scripture quotations marked TEV are from the *Today's English Version* of the New Testament. Copyright © American Bible Society 1966, 1971.

Scripture quotations marked TLB are taken from *The Living Bible, Paraphrased* (Wheaton: Tyndale House Publisher, 1971) and are used by permission.

Scripture quotations marked NASB are from the New American Standard Bible, © The Lockman Foundation, La Habra, Calif., 1960, 1962, 1963. *New American Standard Bible*, New Testament. Published by Broadman Press, Nashville, Tennessee.

Scripture quotations marked Phillips are from *The New Testament in Modern English*, © J. B. Phillips, 1958. Used with permission of the MacMillan Company.

Scripture quotations marked NEB are from *The New English Bible.* © The Delegates of the Oxford University Press, and the Syndics of the Cambridge University Press 1961, 1970. Reprinted by permission.

FOREWORD

You may have been wondering about the fresh winds blowing in the midst of churches and denominations. Here is a book which will give you "on-the-spot" verbalization of these happenings.

The busy pastor and the inquiring lay person will find resource in these pages worth the time to read and study. For most pastors who have interest in renewal, an inadequate supply of sermonic resource and related materials are available. Here it is!

Congregations need preparation for renewal experiences. Bible studies for preparation and testimonies for inspiration are not found in volume. Here it is!

What to do with renewal both in preparation, the event and experience, and the follow-up has needed articulation. Here it is!

I commend to you this wealth of material compiled by the creative direction of a man who has experienced renewal in his life, his church, and his state through evangelism leadership.

C. B. HOGUE, DIRECTOR
Division of Evangelism
Home Mission Board

TO
Betty, Edie, Ed, Melody, Dawn, and Stephane

**My beautiful wife and lovely children who
provide renewal to me every time I come home
from a revival or the office.**

INTRODUCTION

Several years ago when the director of the Texas Evangelism Division assigned me the job of renewal evangelism I was less than enthusiastic. All I knew about renewal was a weekend called Lay Witness Mission. Now I know God was directing that assignment. I learned several interesting facets about renewal. First, renewal, though its roots may be found much earlier, arose in the late 1950's and developed through the decade of the 1960's.

Second, renewal has almost as many definitions as Carter has pills. It means different things to different people. It is a kind of umbrella word that has come to be popular and is used by people to refer to the new that seems to be taking place in religion today. In general, renewal means the work of God in calling his people to new and deeper levels of discipleship. It is a call for all believers to be ministers and for the pastors' ministry to be that of equipping the ministers. Renewal includes an emphasis on the lordship of Christ, on the Spirit-filled life, on believers finding their particular ministry, and on the necessity of witness.

Third, renewal is a description of what God is doing in the world. He is awakening the laity. This awakening is universal and inter-denominational. It was not on anyone's official agenda. It just began. That is an awakening. It is the difference in our doing something and asking God to get with us and in God doing something and asking us to get with him.

Fourth, renewal is a movement that is progressive and involves special programs. In the Southern Baptist Convention it is suggested that churches take their people on a journey that begins with a Lay Renewal Weekend. This weekend is followed by the lay WIN Strategy, the Lay Ministries and Evangelism Weekend, and finally, Lay Revivals. The first weekend is designed to help people on the journey inward. The other three weekends help people take the journey outward. In other words, renewal helps church members learn how to live a life worth sharing and how to share a life worth living.

In working with churches and their pastors, it became evident that pastors often scheduled a renewal weekend without making adequate preparation for the weekend and without planning a thorough follow-up. This book is dedicated to supplying pastors with various types of renewal materials for preaching and for acquainting themselves with renewal concepts.

In talking with lay people, it became evident that many were limited in their concept of renewal to a lay renewal weekend. This book was produced to help them broaden their knowledge of renewal.

Who is the author? God has used men and women from all parts of the United States to write the sermons, Bible studies, illustrations, testimonies, and interpretations. He has been behind the book.

A special word of thanks must go to Reid Hardin, David Haney, and Ras Robinson for their encouragement and guidance. Furthermore, without the capable assistance of Mrs. Ron Bone, Mrs. Dwain Stephens, and Mrs. Larry Roberts the manuscript would not have been typed, proofread, and completed for distribution. We praise God for their courtesies.

GEORGE E. WORRELL

CONTENTS

I SERMONS

1

The Equipping Pastor

David Haney

BROTHERHOOD COMMISSION, SOUTHERN BAPTIST CONVENTION,
MEMPHIS, TENNESSEE

Now a Jew named Apollos, a native of Alexandria, came to Ephesus. He was an eloquent man, well versed in the scriptures. He had been instructed in the way of the Lord; and being fervent in spirit, he spoke and taught accurately the things concerning Jesus, though he knew only the baptism of John. He began to speak boldly in the synagogue; but when Priscilla and Aquila heard him, they took him and expounded to him the way of God more accurately. And when he wished to cross to Achaia, the brethren encouraged him, and wrote to the disciples to receive him. When he arrived, he greatly helped those who through grace had believed, for he powerfully confuted the Jews in public, showing by the scriptures that the Christ was Jesus (Acts 18:24-28, RSV).

Someone has suggested that a good pastor is one who preaches exactly twenty minutes and then sits down. He condemns sin, but never hurts anyone's feelings. He labors from 8:00 A.M. to 10:00 P.M. in every kind of work, from preaching to custodial service. He makes $60 a week, wears good clothes, buys good books regularly, has a nice family, drives a good car, and gives $30 a week to the church. He also stands ready to contribute to every good work that comes along. The ideal pastor is twenty-six years old and has been preaching for thirty years. He is at once tall and short, thin and heavy-set, and handsome. He has one brown eye and one blue; his hair is parted in the middle with left side dark and straight and the right side brown and wavy. He has a burning desire to work with teenagers and spends all his time with the older folks. He smiles all the time with a straight face because he has a sense of humor that keeps him seriously dedicated to his work. He makes fifteen calls a day on church members, spends all his time evangelizing the unchurched, and is never out of his office! [1]

According to the New Testament, the pastor of a church has a *specific* function. It is the standard by which his success or failure is to be determined . . . by the Lord of the church.

The New Testament, however, is not as fuzzy as this culturally accumulated definition. The New Testament says that the pastor is to "equip the saints for the work of the ministry" (Eph. 4:11-12). That is his calling. Yet, as Robert Raines says: "The clergyman's abiding frustration is that in doing the many things that are useful, he may be prevented from doing the one thing needful. It is being suggested here that the one thing needful in the role of the clergyman for our time is that he prepare his people for their ministry in the church and in the world. *The chief task of the clergyman is to equip his people for their ministry.* All his work is to this end. The functions of preacher, prophet, pastor, priest, evangelist, counselor, and administrator find their proper places in the equipping ministry." [2]

According to the Book which is our "authority for faith and practice," every believer has his or her own particular "ministry." Every follower of the Christ has his or her own "calling," his or her own "gift."

> "But *each of us* has been given his gift" (Eph. 4:7, NEB, italics added).
>
> "There are varieties of gifts, but the same Spirit. There are varieties of service, but the same Lord. There are many forms of work, but all of them, *in all men,* are the work of the same God. In *each of us* the Spirit is manifested in one particular way, for some useful purpose" (1 Cor. 12:4-7, NEB, italics added).
>
> "God has given *each of you* some special abilities; be sure to use them to help each other, passing on to others God's many kinds of blessings" (1 Pet. 4:10, TLB, italics added).

In the Old Testament strategy, there was a "priestly tribe" *among* the tribes, the Levites. They were the priests *for* the people. In the New Testament reordering of the strategy, however, we are a "kingdom of priests" (Rev. 1:6). No longer are there those who minister for us; now, we are *all* in the *ministry*.

The *pastor's* ministry in this New Testament strategy is to equip the people for *their* ministries and, believe me, the pastor who takes this biblical assignment as seriously as he does literally is . . . a *new* pastor!

But, what does it mean? How is it done? *What does an "equipper" look like?* Let me suggest that the job which Priscilla and Aquila did on Apollos is a good model of what Christ had in mind for the ministry of "equipping."

Equipping Means Evangelizing

We know precious little about Apollos. He was from Alexandria in Egypt, a Jew well-versed in the Old Testament Scriptures, who arrived in Ephesus and began preaching. Apparently, he had come under the influence of the followers of John the Baptist and had received baptism at their hands. But, he could only preach the "facts about Jesus" (Acts 18:25, NEB). Consequently, Priscilla and Aquila took him underwing and told him the "rest of the story."

If it wasn't such bad theology, we could call Apollos "half saved." That is, he knew the facts . . . but not the Person. What they gave him was the difference in an academic hope and an experienced reality. And, there are many like him . . . today!

Some people are "half in" the church. That is, they are *among* us, but not yet *of* us. They have the facts, but not the faith. They know the language, but not the Lord. In short, they have never been struck with the blinding reality: *He lives!* Apollos *expected* him; Aquila and Priscilla knew that he had come! Apollos knew *about* him; Aquila and Priscilla *knew* him!

Others, however, are "half out" of the church. Like so many today, they are the "disillusioned disciples." Somehow, by God's grace, they know that there *has to be more* to Christianity than merely making up an audience, paying dues, serving on committees, ad infinitum . . . *ad nauseum!* They are asking: "Is this it? Is this all there is?"

And, being turned off, they are turning away . . . sometimes even being turned away!

We begin the "equipping" task when we share the *good news* with these the "half saved": that he is *here* and, yes, there is *more!* The "new pastor" begins there.

Equipping Means Educating

The equipping of Apollos did not end with his evangelizing—as it does all too often today. Someone has said that the last instruction most converts receive after they have come forward in an invitation is to "sit down and fill out this card." Rather, "they took him in hand and expounded the new way to him in greater detail" (Acts 18:26, NEB). While he had the basic elements, they helped him to fill in the blanks and to color in the borders.

The pastor who takes seriously his equipping role in education will take a long look at two things: his *preaching* and his *program*. If his preaching is only "how to be saved—you'd better attend Sunday night—tithe your income," then it is sadly short of the New Testament definition of both "pastor" and "evangelism." Not for nothing does Ephesians 4:11-12 equate "pastor" and "teacher"; and the Great Commission has not been fulfilled until we "make disciples" (learners), "teaching them to observe" all we have been commanded (Matt. 28:19-20).

Likewise, our *programs* are involved. If the people are to be equipped, then they must be taught. But, they must be taught in such a way that they are equipped to *fulfill their ministries*. Our educational structures exist, not for the sake of good *programs*, but for good *products!* It is dangerous (but wise) to ask what we are trying to do with all of our educational programs—and then to see if they are accomplishing it!

Whenever and wherever renewal crops out, a pastor's preaching and program takes on new depth and breadth. He becomes a "new pastor," indeed!

Equipping Means Encouraging

Rather than to "put him down" or "in his place," Aquila and

Priscilla *encouraged* Apollos in his ministry. Rather than to be the sole *torchbearers,* they chose to be *lamplighters.* Whatever else, that alone tells us that they had solved the "ego" problem which hamstrings many a pastor today.

Most of us are more able to emulate Barnabas than Aquila and Priscilla. That is, Barnabas dealt well with another's *failure.* For instance, when John Mark failed as a missionary (Acts 13:13) and turned back, Barnabas reclaimed him. He took Mark back into ranks of the "Foreign Mission Board," even at the cost of severing relationships with Paul (Acts 15:36-40), but wisely so: Mark gave us the first Gospel!

However, it is another thing to deal with one's *success.* Yet, that was the life-style of Aquila and Priscilla. When Paul came to Corinth, they were already there and already entrenched as the leaders of the Christian movement there (Acts 18:1-4). When Paul came, they chose to see him, not as an intruder, but recognizing his gifts, they gave him "stage-center" and encouraged him on. So, too, with Apollos. They simply "polished" him, then stood back and *let him shine!*

In fact, the whole Ephesian church "encouraged him" (Acts 18:27)! (Churches have a way of following the lead of their leaders!) They encouraged him in his ministry at Ephesus and, when he felt called to go to Corinth, they encouraged him again. Who can measure the importance of an encouraging fellowship? Who indeed!

The equipping pastor *evangelizes,* then *educates,* and when the minister emerges, he *encourages.* But, how does one do that? Deliberately.

Equipping Means Engaging

The ultimate goal of equipping is to see the person *engaged* in ministry. You see, Jesus called for laborers, not admirers. The "test" of the pastor has to do with *ministry* he performs and the *ministers* he produces.

That Aquila and Priscilla did an effective work of equipping Apollos is to be seen in the fact that when he arrived in Corinth, "he greatly helped" them (Acts 18:28).

In that sense, Apollos represents a "finished product" of the equipping ministry. Not a perfect product, to be sure; but a finished one. He was evangelized, educated, encouraged, and now he was *engaged!*

Conclusion

It was a turning point in my own pastoral ministry when I began to look at the New Testament standard of success and failure. That is, I began to look at the *products* of it. I found, among other things, that I had produced some crowds, some budgets, some buildings, some acclaim—but few, very few, *ministers!* My biographical data sheet listed a good many accomplishments, but very few "finished products." I wanted to change! I did. Or rather, I'm still in the process and, while the record isn't much to shout about, it is *better.*

I once heard someone say about pastors that "while they are called to be *fishers of men,* they have become *keepers of the aquarium.*" At that time, I thought it was both apt and cute. Now, however, after living with the New Testament standard, I know that it was only cute. We are, indeed, called to be "fishers of men," but we shall be held the more accountable for being, in fact, "keepers of the aquarium."

"And He gave some to be pastors and teachers to equip the saints to do the work of the ministry."

Notes

[1] See the writer's *The Idea of the Laity,* (Grand Rapids: Zondervan, 1972), p. 42.
[2] Robert Raines, *New Life in the Church,* (New York: Harper and Row, 1961), p. 17.

2

The New Laity

Fred H. Wolfe

COTTAGE HILLS BAPTIST CHURCH,
MOBILE, ALABAMA

On every hand we see tired preachers and frustrated laymen. Why? In many cases the preacher is trying to do it all, and he is tired. At the same time, laymen are frustrated because they want to do more.

This was exactly the situation with Moses and the children of Israel in Exodus 18. In Exodus 18:18 we read the words of Moses' father-in-law spoken to Moses: "Thou wilt surely wear away, both thou, and this people that is with thee; this thing is too heavy for thee; thou art not able to perform it thyself alone." Moses' father-in-law instructed Moses to involve other men in carrying out the work of the Lord. God did not intend for Moses to do it all. God desired to use other men.

Down through history God has always used men. From Abraham to Paul to our modern day, God has used men to carry out his earthly ministry. In every critical situation it is a man or group of men who have made the difference for good or bad.

There is excitement abroad because of a new involvement of the laity in the work of the Lord. A minister and a local church multiply their ministry a hundred-fold when lay people are released and renewed to serve the living Lord. The work of the Lord is the work of the *whole church* for the *whole age*.

In the eighteenth chapter of Exodus, we note that while there were plenty of laymen to do the work they were—

Laymen Restricted.

They were not involved in the ministry of the Lord. This has been, and still is, perhaps the most serious problem in our local churches—laymen restricted.

In times past laymen have been restricted by *faulty leadership*.

In Exodus 18, the people were willing but there was no leadership to involve them. This is still true in our day. Faulty leadership is failing to involve willing lay people in the work of the Lord.

Creative leadership in the pulpit and the pew will confront willing lay people with what God expects, commands, and asks of them. Yes, laymen have been restricted by faulty leadership.

Laymen have also been restricted by *false ideas.* The early church described in the book of Acts was a church with total involvement of its people. It was not just the apostles doing the work of the Lord. It was all of the children of God, like flames of fire, sharing and ministering in the name and power of their living Lord. As the whole church moved out in the name of Christ, all of the known world came to know the claims and commands of the risen Lord in less than three hundred years.

Unfortunately, the false ideas of the cleavage of clergy and laity emerged about this time. There began an ever-widening gap between pulpit and pew. The cry seemed to be, "Let the men of the cloth do the work of the Lord." "Leave it to the preacher or the priest." This cry is still heard today. Leave it to the preacher and the staff. They will do the work for the Lord for us. The truth, however, is that no one can serve the Lord in your place. You must serve the Lord as God so wills and chooses for you. *False ideas* have restricted the laity.

This is a new day, however. There is a healthy, heavenly emphasis on the ministry of the total church, and we are seeing it on every hand.

Laymen Released

There is evidence on every hand of a releasing of the layman to serve the Lord. This releasing of the layman to serve his Lord is coming through *prayer.* In Exodus 18:19 Jethro told Moses, "Be thou for the people to God-ward, that thou mayest bring the causes unto God." The prayer on lips of pastor and layman alike today seems to be: Oh, God, raise up your people in the pew to do your work. I sense that we are heeding the words of our blessed Lord,

"Pray ye therefore the Lord of the harvest, that he will send forth labourers unto his harvest" (Matt. 9:38).

Laymen are also being released through *preparation.* In Exodus 18:20 as Moses released the people to the work, we read, "And thou shalt teach them ordinances and laws, and shalt shew them the way wherein they must walk, and the work that they must do." It is the task of the minister of God to equip the saints for the work of the ministry. The reason we continue to have lay evangelism schools, lay renewal weekends, and other training activities is to release the layman to do the work of the Lord through *preparation.*

Laymen are also released by *selection* and *setting apart.* Moses set out in Exodus 18 to select and set apart men to carry on the work of the Lord. How true is the common phrase, "Everybody's business is nobody's business." There must be a *specific* selection and setting apart under the leadership of the Holy Spirit of lay people to places where God desires for them to serve. It is exciting to see lay people released in specific ministries, such as the bus ministry, prison ministry, prayer ministry, outreach ministry, and lay renewal ministry.

We are seeing today not only the releasing of the layman, but also, in a great and glorious way, we are seeing—

Laymen Renewed.

It is not enough for restrictions on laymen to be removed, and for there to be a release to serve the Lord. There must also be *spiritual renewal.* How often have we heard the words, *"What we are is more important than what we do. For what we are determines what we do."* It is not just doing, it is being.

Renewal comes in and through the Holy Spirit. We need to hear again the words of Zechariah 4:6, "Not by might, nor by power, but by my spirit, saith the Lord of hosts." Might and power in this great verse represent human resources, and it is clear that they are *not enough* unless they are empowered by *his Spirit.* We are engaged in a spiritual battle, and as laymen are released to do the Lord's work they must be renewed by his Spirit. How his precious word in Ephesians 6:10 needs to be heeded, "Be strong in the Lord, and in the power of his might."

Renewal comes to lay people through *instruction*. We must be taught to *work in the Spirit*. We have made much, and rightfully so, of the plan of salvation. On the other hand, we have made far too little of walking and living in the Spirit. Only as the Holy Spirit fills and works uniquely through our personalities will lay renewal be a reality.

Renewal also comes through *submission*. As we, laymen and pastors alike, come with our unique God-given abilities and talents and place them on the altar in submission to Christ as Lord, we will experience real renewal. On every hand today we see laymen being instructed and coming in submission to Jesus as Lord. Lay renewal is a reality in our day.

Renewal, likewise, comes through *appropriation* of our resources in Christ. How true the words in Colossians 2:9-10: "For in him dwelleth all the fulness of the Godhead bodily. And *ye are complete in him*, which is the head of all principality and power" (italics added). As Christ Jesus the Lord lives in us and through us, we can exclaim with Paul, in Philippians 4:13, "I can do all things through Christ which strengtheneth me."

Conclusion

Unrestricted, released and renewed laymen bring fresh and new excitement and power to the church of Jesus Christ. The future is both exciting and breathtaking.

Renewal is the in-thing. It is an idea whose time has come. Recognizing the lordship of Christ, laymen are demanding a part of the action. They realize that there is more to being a Christian than voting yes on all the recommendations that come from the deacons and church committees. They are no longer willing for the preacher to have all the joy of sharing Christ with the lost. They are fearful, but they are determined to witness at work, in their homes and communities. Laymen no longer look at the church as organized and functioning for itself. They look at it as a springboard for service and sharing. Some are carrying their faith into the fields of politics, education, medicine, and science. Their renewal is making a difference in their homes, children, and their own moral lives.

Because of God's movement among laymen, I agree with the words I heard Manley Beasley speak in recent days, "All over the land God is placing small puddles of renewal and renewed people, and soon God is going to bring all these puddles together to form a mighty river of revival sweeping away every obstacle in its path."

Praise the Lord! Lay renewal is a reality.

3

Spiritual Gifts for Ministry

Emory Wallace

FIRST BAPTIST CHURCH,
DERIDDER, LOUISIANA

Suppose some angelic being who since the beginning of creation had dwelt in the presence of God would suddenly appear on earth and live among us for a while. Do you not imagine that he would be astonished at what he would see? He would surely wonder how we Christians could be contented with our commonplace level of experience.

If this angelic being knew such blazing personalities as Moses, David, Isaiah, Paul, Stephen, Augustine, Brainard, and others, he might logically conclude that twentieth-century Christians had either misunderstood some vital doctrine of the faith or had stopped short of the true acquaintance with God.

Perhaps the angelic visitor would ask himself: "Where is the spiritual power that has been so manifest among God's people in other days? Where are the gifts of the Spirit which make Christians instruments that God can use and conduits through which the gospel of free grace can flow?"

Our Lord has made adequate provision for us to become the people of God he saved us to be and to accomplish the task for which he commissioned us. God never intended for "us" to do "his" work, or for "us" to be able to live "his" (the Christian) life. This provision comes in the form of what is called spiritual gifts.

This message is a study of the endowment God has bestowed upon every Christian through spiritual gifts.

The Endowment Provided

There is much misunderstanding and misinformation concerning spiritual gifts. This seems to have been true through the ages. It was especially true at Corinth about A.D. 55 among the Christian believers. Paul wrote at length in his first epistle to the Corinthians concerning spiritual gifts (1 Cor. 12—14).

Paul begins 1 Corinthians 12 with the words, "Now concerning spiritual gifts, brethren, I would not have you ignorant." He is not talking about ignorance of the fact of spiritual gifts but rather ignorance of the purpose of these gifts. The Corinthian Christians seemed to be well informed that they possessed spiritual gifts, but they were ignorant about the use of them. "They were using their God-given tools like toys. They wrote up their own job description out of their experiences."

Paul and other biblical writers present us with some general truths concerning spiritual gifts.

Gifts are sovereignly bestowed (1 Cor. 12:11). The Holy Spirit gives the gifts in the context of his strategy for the church. He distributes to each believer a gift or gifts that he wishes us to have. Christians are not to pray for any specific gift. Rather the Holy Spirit "as he will" bestows them upon members of the body of Christ. We do not earn them. We certainly do not deserve them. They are gifts "allotted to us by God's grace and must be exercised accordingly" (Rom. 12:6, NEB). Since these gifts are sovereignly given by the Holy Spirit, there is no reason for jealousy among the members of the Lord's church.

A spiritual gift is not a natural talent but a manifestation of the Holy Spirit. God may use a person's natural talent in the exercising of some gift. However, spiritual gifts are supernaturally bestowed, and one does not have them before they become a Christian. Even after one has been converted, these gifts may not be recognized immediately. In some cases they lie dormant in a person's life for long periods of time. Today God is using the process of renewal in the body of Christ to awaken believers to the fact that they have latent spiritual gifts.

Thus the church is Christ's body and is made up of "gifted members." Christ is the head of this body. This means that the church is an extension of the life and ministry of our Lord in our generation. If the church is to minister effectively, all members of the body must discover their gifts and begin exercising those gifts in some spiritual ministry.

First Peter 4:10-11 provides a good general summary of the spiritual gifts. It emphasizes the fact that every Christian has a gift or gifts with which to minister in the body of Christ. For these "gifts of grace" to be effectively used they must be exercised in the power of the Holy Spirit. The end result is "that God in all things may be glorified through Jesus Christ."

The church at Corinth is a classic example of the ineffective use of spiritual gifts. This church had all the gifts (1 Cor. 1:7) yet was one of the most carnal churches in history. The mere possession of spiritual gifts does not insure spirituality. For a spiritual gift to bear spiritual fruit, it must be exercised by a spirit-filled believer.

Ephesians 4:11-12 sets forth the special assignment for the pastor of the church. God says that each member of the body ought to be engaging in works of service. It is the pastor's responsibility to prepare God's people for these works of service. The God-called pastor has been especially gifted by the Holy Spirit to accomplish his assigned task. That task includes equipping the members for their spiritual ministry; helping them discover their gifts; and developing them properly in the service of their Lord.

Elton Trueblood refers to the pastor as the "player-coach." When we think of this term we think of the great Bill Russell, who for several years was the player-coach of the Boston Celtics. It was his responsibility as player-coach to train the team in all of the intricacies of the game and to see to it that each man was equipped to do his best when game time arrived. Then the player-coach, having taught the men as best he could, got out on the court with them and played the game with his team. So it is with the player-coach in the church. The pastor has been called and endowed by God with special gifts to equip the members of the body in order that the God-given gifts they possess can be used to the maximum for the Lord Jesus.

The Endowment Defined

In the Scriptures there are different gifts listed. Various groupings have been suggested for these gifts. Generally they fall into three categories including the sign, speaking, and serving gifts.

The *sign gifts* include miracles, healings, tongues, and interpretation of tongues. Most Baptist and evangelical Christians believe that these gifts were temporary gifts. Earl Radmacher, president of Western Conservation Seminary in Portland, Oregon, in a lecture on spiritual gifts and Ralph Neighbour, Jr., in his book, *This Gift Is Mine*, both make very sound and convincing arguments from the Scriptures that these sign gifts were given by God to the early church to authenticate the message of the gospel to the world. They also existed to establish a testimony especially to the Jews that Christians were indeed the people of God (1 Cor. 14:22).

The emphasis that Paul makes in 1 Corinthians 12 is that where you have a spiritual manifestation of spiritual gifts, you will have growing unity. It is easy to see that some of the things that are going on today in the name of spiritual gifts which produce divisiveness and schism cannot be of God. Seldom is there any disagreement or divisiveness in the church because of one of the speaking or serving gifts. It is the sign gifts that cause confusion. You never hear of a church being split over someone exercising the gift of helps, or the gift of faith, or the gift of giving. As Ralph Neighbour says, "The eleven service gifts quietly manifest themselves in a divine flow within the body life." The four sign gifts are anything but quiet. They attract attention to themselves. When they do, they detract from the blessed head of the body. As someone has said, "To have a great encounter with God and to come away enamored with the experience rather than with God is sophisticated adultery. We are not to magnify the gift instead of the giver. We are not to go out as an evangel for our gifts. We are to go out as an evangel for God."

As one thinks of the whole concept of spiritual gifts, we must not short-circuit our effectiveness by failing to use the gifts that God has provided or by abusing what he has given us by accepting a counterfeit from Satan. Satan works both ways. If he cannot get us to ignore the good things God has provided for the ongoing of

the church, he will try to get us to pervert the things that we have
been given.

The *speaking gifts* are five in number. First there is the gift of
prophecy (preaching) (1 Cor. 14:1). This supreme gift signifies the
opening of the Scriptures to tell forth the word and wisdom of God.
The prophet or the preacher was and is a mouthpiece for God.
He is not to innovate or philosophize but to communicate the truth
of God. It is well to note that this gift has not been given exclusively
to those who are preachers by vocation. Many laymen have the
gift of preaching.

Second, there is the gift of *teaching* (Rom. 12:7). There is a difference in preaching and teaching. The preacher stands and an-
nounces the truth of God, while teaching is more dialogue. It involves
the listeners in the presentation of truth. One with the gift of teaching
communicates well and passes truth on in learnable forms. This gift
is not limited to prophets, evangelists, and pastor-teachers. In every
church God has equipped the body with lay people who have the
gift of teaching. In every church there are enough God-equipped
teachers to care for the needs of that congregation.

Third is the gift of *knowledge* (1 Cor. 12:8). The person with
this gift finds his most comfortable place in a study surrounded by
books. God has given this person the ability to mine spiritual truths
from the word of God systematizing these truths and making them
available to others for use.

Fourth is the gift of *wisdom* (1 Cor. 12:8). The person who has
been given the gift of wisdom has the ability to apply the great
principles of Scripture to problems in such clear ways that all can
see the answers. Perhaps Solomon in the Old Testament portrayed
this gift when he commanded that a baby be split so that each of
the two women who claimed it could have a part. Of course the
real mother protested, giving up her claim to the baby in order
that it might live. Solomon then ruled that she was to have the
infant. Another incident may be seen in Acts 15:13 where James
applied wisdom to smooth out a knotty problem experienced in the
Jerusalem church. The person with this gift might have difficulty

digging the truths from God's Word but when someone else has done this they are able to take the truth and make the practical applications.

Last there is the gift of *exhortation* (Rom. 12:8). The one with this gift is not the person who urges us to make a commitment but rather one who has the unusual gift of counseling, encouraging, and reassuring people. The word exhortation comes from *parakaleo*. Barnabas, with his wonderful experience of salvaging the life of John Mark, is an excellent example of one who had this great gift. As a young man, John Mark disappointed the great apostle Paul. After time spent in service with Barnabas, Mark matured to the extent that Paul requested that Mark be sent to help him in the ministry (2 Tim. 4:11).

The *service gifts* are found in Romans 12 and 1 Corinthians 12. There are six gifts that might be called service gifts. The gift of *faith* is mentioned in 1 Corinthians 12:9. All Christians have faith as a gift from God. Without it none could come to Christ (Eph. 2:8-9). However, some in the body of Christ have been given a gift of faith that is beyond the faith that brings salvation. Some have called this gift a gift of "vision." This person has the ability to see what the Lord is able and willing to do above and beyond that which most others in the body are able to see.

Christian history is filled with such men and women. One of the greatest was George Mueller. He acknowledged that he had the gift of faith. During his lifetime George Mueller prayed and more than thirteen million dollars were given, but he never had more than the equivalent of sixty pounds in the bank at any one time. Once he and the children in one of his orphanages gathered around the tables at their empty plates. They thanked the Lord for that which they were about to receive. Then a milkman knocked on the door and said, "My wagon just broke down out there and the milk is going to spoil. Could you use it?" "Well, as a matter of fact we could," said Mueller, "we just thanked the Lord for it."

A more recent example of God's bestowing the gift of faith upon a person is found in the life of Cameron Townsend who founded the Wycliffe Bible Translators, Incorporated. In 1934 he envisioned a school and an organization to train young people to translate the word of God into the thousands of languages in the world. The vision of Cameron Townsend was to have the Word of God translated into every language and dialect in the world by A.D. 2000. Hundreds of young people have entered the vision of this man of faith.

In every church there are those with the gift of faith. Members of the body ought to heed these when they project ministries and programs even though, humanly speaking, such ministries might seem impossible.

Other service gifts includes gifts of helps (1 Cor. 12:28) or *ministry* (Rom. 12:7). The gift of faith mentioned above may be more dramatic than this gift. However, for the vision that faith brings to become a reality there is need for the gift of helps or ministry. The person with this gift has the ability to lend a hand wherever any need appears and to do it in such a way that it strengthens and encourages others spiritually. This is perhaps the most common gift among members of the body. The church could not operate without many exercising this gift. This gift is evident in some deacons, ushers, treasurers, those who prepare the Lord's Supper elements, those who arrange flowers, and those who serve dinners.

The gift of *discernment* is mentioned in 1 Corinthians 12:10. While the gift of faith is the gift of enablement for the church, the gift of discernment is a gift of protection for the church. This gift enables one to tell the difference between the spirit of error and truth before the difference brings hurt and harm to the church. In Acts 5, Simon Peter perceived that Ananias and Sapphira had lied against the Holy Spirit. Most of us probably would never have seen the spirit of hypocrisy manifested here because of the large gift they brought. Simon Peter having the gift of discernment immediately said, "This is of the devil." The gift of discernment is vital in protecting the church in our day when heresy and error abound on every hand.

The gift of administration or *service* is found in Romans 12:7. The word service describes one who serves. It is the word used by unhappy Martha when she said to Jesus in Luke 10:40 (NEB), "Lord, do you not care that my sister has left me to get on with the work by myself." The one with this gift delights in the privilege of serving other members of the family of God. Recently some women in our church have driven 110 miles a day for six weeks to take a fellow member to a hospital for cobalt treatments. A deacon mows a widow's lawn and has done so for years without being asked and without notice. He is serving another member of the body.

Romans 12:8 sets forth the gift of *giving*. The word giving comes from the Greek word meaning "to share with." Thus the gift of giving is direct reference to the material things of life. It means to share with others material resources including food, clothing, or money. Every Christian has a stewardship responsibility to his Lord but the person with this gift has an unusual desire to give to the work of God. R. G. LeTourneau who gave 90 percent of all that he earned is an example of one whom God endowed to earn money and upon whom the Lord bestowed the gift of giving. The Lord also bestows this gift upon those who are less able to give. The Macedonian Christians seemed to have had this gift for they gave generously far beyond that which they could be expected to give (2 Cor. 8:1-5).

Finally, there is the gift of *leadership* in Romans 12:8. There are some in the body upon whom the Lord has bestowed the gift of leadership. These have a spiritual capacity to be obedient to Christ. Ralph Neighbour adequately describes this gift when he says: "The leadership gift does not have to do with goals and committees, it is the man who has been with God, who has been dealt with by the spirit of God. He is like Moses when he comes down from the mountain. The body recognizes his authority to lead, his commitment to the Lord's calling is as deep as his heartbeat. Murmuring, disappointment, and feeling alone will not slow him down. He leads others, not on the basis of talents, but from a total obedience to the call of God."

There they are, eleven gifts that manifest themselves in the body of Christ. You are there someplace! You are found in these eleven gifts. Every member of the body of Christ has one or more of these spiritual gifts for service, ready to be developed and used.

The Endowment Discovered

Many Christians have lived for years without being aware of the spiritual gifts which are theirs. What are the principles of discovery? How can Christians recognize and discover their spiritual gifts?

First, learn what the Scripture teaches concerning spiritual gifts. God has a gift or a cluster of gifts for every believer and he desires to reveal them to us that we may begin exercising these gifts in ministry for him.

Second, walk in submission to the Lord. He will reveal the good things to us and give us the desires of our heart. There also must be a willingness to receive in sweet humility what the sovereign God has for us. Not wishing for some other gift but gladly receiving that which he has for us.

Third, as soon as one begins to sense what their gift is, they should begin exercising that gift and seeking to develop it. As one grows in prayer and spiritual maturity the gift will be enhanced and other gifts will likely be revealed.

Last, as we fellowship with other Christians and participate in group sharing, fellow Christians will notice gifts or potential gifts in our lives many times before they are known by us. Others see us often better than we see ourselves. In a spiritually-minded body of believers, they will affirm in us the spiritual gifts they see.

Conclusion

These gifts are the fundamental provisions of the Lord for the operation of his body and church. Pity the church which fails to understand this and substitutes instead the business methods, organizational proceedings, and pressure politics of the world to accomplish the work.[1]

God has equipped the church to use its gifts for ministry. The church should use them!

Notes
[1] Ray Stedman, *Body Life*, (Glendale: Regal, 1952), p. 51.

4

The Ministry Is for the Laity

Lewis Abbot

FIRST BAPTIST CHURCH,
NORCROSS, GEORGIA

Recently a middle-aged man sat in my study sharing his conversion experience and expressing a deep desire to learn how to lead others to Christ. He said, "I know that God has called me to minister but I am not equipped. Will you help me learn how to do what God wants me to do?" Charles Holbrook is a prime example of thousands of lay people who are longing for the equipping ministry of the church.

The equipping ministry is the responsibility Christ gave to pastor-teachers and is illustrated by his question-and-answer session with Peter. In John 21:15-17 Jesus asked Peter three times, "Do you love me?" Peter responded, "Yes, Lord." Then Jesus said, "Feed my sheep." Jesus has charged us in Matthew 28:18-20 to "make disciples" out of believers. All believers are to be disciples. Every disciple is a "called" servant of God to be an "ambassador for Christ," reconciling men to God by being life-style evangelists sharing the beautiful love of Jesus with a broken defeated humanity. Today there is a sweeping grass-roots movement of God's Spirit among the people of God growing out of a hunger and thirst for a deeper, more fulfilling and fruitful life in Christ. A growing crescendo of voices is calling for a new ministry—a new or renewed direction for the ministry as found in God's word.

The church is the commissioned agent of God to bring into being and maintain a dynamic style of life and ministry that can transform lives. The gospel message must find expression in the life of the church. The structures of the church are under a divine imperative to serve the needs of the body of Christ by equipping the body for its new ministry. There are four specific components vital to such a new ministry: some new concepts, a new call, a new climate, and a new commitment.

Some New Concepts

The new concepts which move the people of God toward ministry include the church as the innkeeper and all Christians as ministers. First note the church as the innkeeper. D. T. Niles, the eloquent preacher from Ceylon, suggested the true imagery of the good Samaritan story. He pointed out Christians are not the Samaritans searching for battered humanity to bring them to wholeness. Rather Christians are to be the innkeepers. Jesus is the Samaritan. He finds the battered person. He trusts us with him. We become innkeepers as laborers together with God. Innovative ministries are the result.[1]

The second concept is that of all Christians being commissioned as full-time innkeepers and ministers. This is foreign to modern church belief or practice. Yet the renewal of good news is that Christ transforms our lives on a continuing basis until we become full grown men and women equipped for his ministry in the world. In Ephesians 4:1, Paul says, "Walk worthy of the vocation wherein ye are called." We, as God's children, are given a new vocation which is to be the number one priority of life for all believers. This is true because vocation is the primary emphasis in life. The Christian vocation encompasses the lordship of Christ as one allows him to dominate and control the entire spectrum of life.

The ministry is for all believers and is to be in the world outside the institutional structures we so formally call the church. To qualify as the church, we must be walking step by step with Jesus Christ into our vocation of reconciling the world unto God. This concept of a personal relationship and a ministry of God's servants is beautifully illustrated in the life of Gay Settles.

Six years ago I became Mr. Settles' pastor in Tampa, Florida. Soon he began to come to grips with God's call to a spiritual vocation. Within a year, Mr. Settles was witnessing daily in a new and dynamic style of life. His job at the telephone company became an outpost for Christ. Five years later he retired and is now working full time with our church staff as coordinator of lay ministries. Repeatedly he says, "I am more fulfilled in my spiritual life than ever before." He is presently coordinating the ministries of some two hundred adults as life-style evangelism is becoming a reality. In the past two weeks fifteen persons have accepted Christ as a result of these ministries. Each of the ministries has been born out of a new or rediscovered concept that includes a personal ministry to others with nothing demanded in return.

Jesus demonstrated the concept of life-style evangelism of ministry by going to the people with a life of caring for personal needs. He also closely tied the lives of his followers to the same concept when in John he said, "As the Father hath sent me even so send I you." If renewal is to become a live option in our highly complex society, the people of God must grasp the truth embodied in Jesus' statement. This vital yet so often ignored precept simply means that each individual Christian is to become the incarnate love of God to such an extent that he is willing to spend himself for the physical and spiritual needs of others.

Recently in a class on practical ministries where this new concept was being expounded, a lady said, "It takes a while to understand and believe this. I am going to need some time and help to unlearn some old ways of thinking. I feel unsure and afraid as I contemplate the dramatic changes that could come in my life if I dare apply this concept." The lady was voicing a fear and apprehension thousands of laymen and pastors experience as they apply Jesus' commission of ministry to the secure, oiled structures that serve the church so well but ignore the world outside. A warning is appropriate. A church does not grow by simply creating innovative ministries. A growing organism of a living fellowship serving Christ by meeting the needs of people becomes an innovative church. If a new ministry is to unfold for the twentieth-century church, the directing of our Lord must become an imperative command regardless of the cost and risks involved. The basis of an innovative personal ministry is a personal call from our Lord.

A New Call

All believers are called of God into a vocation of life-style evangelism and ministry. Examine that call in the light of its content and meaning. In Matthew 4:18-19 Jesus sees Peter and Andrew fishing on the Sea of Galilee and calls, "Follow me, and I will make you fishers of men." He said simply, "Follow me," wherever I go. Into the world about him, he plunged head-long, touching the leper and making him well, healing the blind man beside the pool, forgiving the prostitute, healing the crippled man, dialoguing with the Pharisees and other religious leaders, challenging the tired customs of his day that enslaved the spiritual side of men. As he went from town to town, he taught repentance and the coming judgment of God on sin.

It is to this style of life and ministry that Christians have been called. Our ministry comes into fruition as we listen and respond to his voice, "Follow me." Following Jesus is a radical departure from the norm of life. Through our response to his call life becomes a never-ending adventure of discovery of self and others. It becomes more blessed to give than to receive. Life takes the shape of joy and abundance through giving and doing for others in order that they might know the wholeness and love Jesus has for them.

Sometimes our fellowship leads to unexpected places. Recently when a deacon came forward to give his testimony in a sharing time at the evening worship hour, he related to the congregation how he had allowed his real estate business to become his god. As the Lord dealt with him, he had become convicted that God wanted his real estate business. As a result of his commitment to follow Jesus, this man has a growing awareness of an unfolding ministry that continues to take new shapes and forms. He has now purchased a $60,000 piece of property to be used by the church as a renewal retreat center and a home for drop-out teenagers.

Two weeks ago a beautiful young mother began to follow Jesus into the ministry of personal evangelism through the use of evangelistic coffees. These coffees have resulted in six persons accepting Christ as Savior.

Last fall a middle-aged school teacher said, "God is calling me to leave my job and give my full time to his work." Today she teaches a large Sunday School class of ladies, leads the good news clubs in different neighborhoods, and participates in occasional renewal weekends throughout the state.

There are presently forty-three ministry groups functioning in our congregation, all led by persons who have responded to the call of Jesus to life-style evangelism and ministry. When one dares to leave the nets and follow the master, life becomes an ever-changing series of events that challenges one's whole being. Our church is but one of several notable churches participating in various ministries. First Baptist Church, San Antonio is a good example. Eleven of their ministries include the volunteers of love, a clothing ministry, an adult basic learning enrichment ministry, the call ministry, the street ministry, the bus ministry, the international ministry, marriage enrichment group ministry, mobile recreation units, television ministry, and venture missions.[2]

Another ministering church is the Second Baptist Church, Little Rock, Arkansas. Their ministry has many faces. There is a day care center for preschool children and day camp during the summer for first through sixth grades, a free medical clinic for the poor, and Christian psychological services for those who need testing and counseling, a single adult Bible fellowship, a weekly meeting with parents without partners, a Bible study fellowship for unwed mothers, mothers' classes in nutrition, family planning and sewing, girls' clubs and boys' clubs, special tutoring, a clothing room as well as a food pantry, a residence hotel for the retired, a Christian family outdoor recreation program, a Christian art center providing music and drama, the regular Baptist programs with youth, music, and Christian education, and creative worship. All of these ministries reach out to people with the Christian gospel.

A New Climate

Jesus' call is to follow and allow him to make us innkeepers and ministers. Much of the time our lives have been punctuated with constantly repeated efforts on our part to make ourselves fishers of men. In an effort to obey our Savior, we continue to frustrate God's plan for life by running off in all directions to show him how much we can do. We fail to grasp the vision of allowing him to change us through fellowship with himself and his followers.

The climate hinges on our allowing Jesus to remake both our inward lives and our outward relationships. The inner change and the outer relationship take place simultaneously as one "walks in the light" of Jesus day by day and experiences the fellowship of the body. Jesus' call was to a spiritual climate composed of a deep sharing of life, prayer, Jesus' teachings, and preparation for ministry. This godly climate has to be born in the heart of a man, usually the pastor.

> Churches rally to the leadership of a preaching pastor. The pastor is a pace-setter, both for the church family and for the family of ministers. Therefore, there must be a declaration of purpose. The pastor must have some dream or vision of what he sees the congregation's direction to be. Equipping the laity is not only a good thing; it is essential. But laity needs leadership. The pastor is the man God calls to be the pace-setter for the ministers in the pew. His vision must be shared; it must be shared over and over again. The vision of a serving family must grip his spirit. He must understand that the family of faith is to be related to that kind of life-style and declare it.[3]

A second method by which the pastor can create a spiritual climate for ministering is through the work of a small group of followers. Jesus proved the validity and imperative need for the small group. For too long the church has denied the Jesus method of developing a spiritual climate through a vulnerable style of preaching, teaching, and interaction in large and small groups of believers.

The prayer life of the church must likewise be patterned on Jesus' example. He prayed *with* his disciples and alone he prayed *for* them and their needs (note John 17:1 ff).

People everywhere ache for a word with God and from God. The new ministry that is so urgently needed for our day can be nurtured into being through learning how to bare our hearts to God in the fellowship of his people. Ritual and form must be abandoned and God's people taught how to pray. This new dimension of prayer calls for a conversational style of interaction with God and an honest sharing of the real issues that confront us day by day. For his disciples, Jesus' teachings came to life in full color as by precept and example he lived out his teachings in the crucible of difficult situations.

The teachings of Jesus are given strength, direction, and power as they become a part of the teacher and are taught through relational Bible study and dialogue. The whys and hows are to be dealt with out of life's experiences. Such a climate in our church has allowed a man recently to declare that he felt God was leading him to use Wednesday nights to witness in a large mobile home park where he and other team members have a house church on Sunday mornings. Rather than feeling threatened, the church body was free to release him to this ministry even though it involved the "sacred" times of Sunday morning and Wednesday evening.

A New Commitment

Jesus led his following of ordinary folk to see the need of total commitment. As he led them into a deepening understanding of God's great love, he helped them grasp that a man can lose his life if he seeks to save it but that he will save his life if he loses it. He told them to deny their own desires and drives to take up their crosses and follow him. They had no idea where he would lead them nor what the outcome would be, but they followed because they knew him. They loved him, and they loved one another. They were a fellowship of ordinary people who were nurtured into a dynamic, self-abandoned commitment to God. That commitment was an open agenda that said with their lives, "Wherever he leads I will follow, whatever he says I will obey, and whatever he wants from me he can have." They committed their entire lives, and God exploded a new ministry.

During this past year I have seen men and women come to life like popcorn popping as they were enrolled and taught in a year-long course called "A Journey into Discipleship." One lady who is quiet and shy has discovered the gift of evangelism and has led nine persons to Christ in the past month. Another person began a ministry of prayer in the local high school which led to three hundred youth meeting for prayer. A retired deacon now gives his full time to helping others implement their ministries.

All of these people had to grow to the place of saying, "Lord, I am willing to commit my life. I am willing to search, try, fail, and rejoice as I seek your will and ministry for my life."

The foundation of a new ministry is a total commitment that is willing to challenge the customs and norms which have caused churches to become sterile. The new ministry fleshed out in the lives of God's people will tear down the walls and partitions that separate us from one another. A new fellowship will produce new ways of taking Christ's love and compassion to a broken world. The great commission will become a living reality rather than an unattainable ideal. God's love through Jesus will become incarnate in your life. The new ministry is *your* ministry.

Notes

[1] Jimmy R. Allen, "A Society of Innkeepers," *Southwestern Journal of Theology*, (Southwestern Baptist Theological Seminary, Ft. Worth), p. 9.

[2] *Ibid.*, pp. 14-18.

[3] *Ibid.*, p. 11.

5

The New Evangelism

Roy Fish

SOUTHWESTERN BAPTIST THEOLOGICAL SEMINARY,
FORT WORTH, TEXAS

"I am made all things to all men, that I might by all means save some" (1 Cor. 9:22).

It is an encouraging sign that once again evangelism is in the air. It's even more encouraging that in some areas it's being brought down to earth. Periodically there's a necessity of clearing the air as to what evangelism really is, since this beautiful word is actually one of the most abused words in modern vocabulary. The secular press uses the word to describe efforts to persuade people to do things they really don't want to do. Many religious minds would say that everything the church does is evangelism. Some would say that mere "presence" with people in need is evangelism. Others say that there's no distinction between evangelism and social reconstruction. Dick Shepherd poignantly says that to some it has been reduced to the motto, "Be kind to grannie and to the cat."

Consequently, when one speaks or writes about "the new evangelism," there might be justification for laboring the point of definition. In the last ten years there have been a number of "new evangelisms." For instance a national news magazine, in the mid 1960's said, "The new approach to evangelism—visible in such unstructured ministries as coffee homes, industrial missions, and missions to drag strips, ski resorts and 'night people'—is primarily interested not in selling Christianity but in sympathetically expressing a human concern for others." Referring to a "new" evangelism, one professor of religion said at a council on evangelism in 1965, "I abhor the notion of individual salvation. Seeking to save an individual's soul is not evangelism and is no longer even Christian." The secretary of evangelism of an American denomination said, "the redemption of the world is not dependent upon the souls we win for Christ . . . there cannot be individual salvation . . . salvation has more to do with the whole society than with the individual's soul. . . . We must not be satisfied to win people one by one. . . . *Contemporary evangelism* (mine) is moving away from winning souls one by one to the evangelization of the structures of society." Because what has been called the "new evangelism" or "contemporary evangelism" in these instances is not evangelism at all, extreme care must be given when one begins a message on this subject.

Any new evangelism, to be real evangelism, must contain certain features of the old evangelism. For instance, evangelism must always be related to sharing a message. This message is the good news of the saving acts of God in Christ. The cross, the resurrection, and man's response of repentance and faith are integral parts of the message of evangelism. There is no evangelism without the evangel, the good news of God's redeeming love in Christ. A new evangelism which does not contain the old message is nothing short of heresy.

But within the structure of sharing this message, there is room for the new. There certainly will be new methods of evangelism. Feasibly a new spirit of evangelism is always possible. One thing must be settled firmly in our thinking. That is, evangelism is basically the sharing of a message and anything less than this takes us below an irreducible minimum.

What is there in today's evangelism which might be different from that of another generation? What is "new" about the new evangelism?

Evangelism with a New Strategy

Admittedly, the word "new" is inappropriate to describe the strategy of evangelism envisioned by many evangelicals today. Actually, it is more of a rediscovery of a strategy which is over nineteen hundred years old. But in many circles, it is virtually a new strategy.

A part of the new strategy is suggested in a renewal theme, "total penetration through total participation." Actually this describes two aspects of the strategy given by Jesus immediately before his ascension. "Ye shall receive power after that the Holy Ghost has come upon you; and ye shall be witnesses unto me both in Jerusalem and in all Judea, and in Samaria, and unto the uttermost part of the earth" (Acts 1:8).

In Lausanne, Switzerland, in the summer of 1974, some three thousand delegates from almost every country in the world met in a Congress on World Evangelization. Frequently, delegates were challenged in terms of "evangelizing the world in this generation." This means nothing less than every individual in our present world hearing the gospel and having a chance to believe. Though there are formidable obstacles to total penetration of our entire world with the gospel, this must not keep us from thinking in terms of every person in the world hearing of Jesus and his offer of life. There were formidable obstacles when Jesus gave his church this commission nineteen centuries ago. If it seems more idealistic than realistic, we must never forget that the "ideal" was given to us by the risen Lord himself.

Among those who are taking the ideal seriously is E. V. Hill, pastor of the Mt. Zion Baptist Church, in south central Los Angeles. Through the World Christian Training Center, a systematic effort is being made to reach the four hundred thousand people of this section of sprawling Los Angeles. Block-captains, thoroughly trained and equipped, are undertaking the prodigious task of getting the message of Jesus to every individual in this heavily populated area. Already, tens of thousands of people have had the gospel shared with them and several thousand have committed their lives to Christ. This program is involving many churches and hundreds of Christians in an effort toward total penetration.

The resources are at our disposal for world evangelization. The printing press, radio, films, television, and possibly Christian communication's satellites are in our hands. If a commercial soft drink enterprise can mobilize resources with a view to seeing that every person in the world has the opportunity of tasting its beverage, is it too much for the church to think in terms of every person in the world having a chance to *know* of *living* water.

God has always had the entire world on his heart. Total penetration has always been a part of his strategy. But there will never be anything that approximates total penetration of the world apart from something which approximates total participation on the part of the church. His plan is the whole world hearing through the whole church sharing.

Though the church is still terribly far from total participation, giant strides have been made in the last decade in this direction. WIN schools or lay evangelism schools have trained more Southern Baptist laymen for evangelism than any method ever before attempted in that denomination. Coral Ridge Presbyterian Church of Fort Lauderdale, Florida, with its "evangelism explosion" has crossed denominational lines and has been the source of equipping thousands of laymen. Campus Crusade for Christ Institutes have done the same. The Home Mission Board and Brotherhood's Lay Ministries and Evangelism Weekend is designed to help laymen discover their gifts, minister to outsiders, and witness as they go! Mobilization of the church for evangelism has finally assumed a place of top priority in an increasing number of circles.

Evangelism with a New Sensitivity

One of the most revealing statements about the evangelistic method of one of the greatest evangelists of all time is found in 1 Corinthians 9:22: "I am made all things to all men that I might by all means save some." It is reflective of the beautiful element of sensitivity which characterized the evangelism of the apostle Paul.

Something of a revival of sensitivity seems to be taking place in evangelism today. Of course, being sensitive to the fact that other people have deep needs has always been a factor in true evangelism. This kind of "general sensitivity" has characterized evangelistic efforts of all types for all time. But the kind of sensitivity I am talking about is more than a general awareness of the fact that people have needs. It is sensitivity at the point of a person's particular need and further to a person's feeling about being approached concerning that need.

At the Lausanne meeting of 1974, one of the most appreciated and best attended conferences was one called "cross-cultural evangelism." One of the major papers was entitled, "The Highest Priority:

Cross-Cultural Evangelism." The thrust of both was the vital necessity of being aware of where people are in their thinking as we attempt to take the good news to them. I believe it is a reflection of an increased emphasis on perception of particular needs of people with whom we need to share.

Though the content of the gospel is not to be compromised, we must be willing "to become all things to all men" in sharing that gospel. Perhaps one of the weaknesses of some evangelism of the past has been the effort to superimpose the same preconceived method and technique on every witnessing situation. We have not been willing to find out where people are. There may have been times when we were too eager to speak and not willing enough to listen. We have failed to realize at times, that every person exercises the privilege of being different from anyone else. People come in many shapes and sizes. The same suit will not fit them all. Sensitivity will keep us aware of this and will compel us to understand as much about a person as possible in our effort to reach that person for Christ.

This renewal of sensitivity has led some churches to think in terms of "Target Group" evangelism. This calls attention to people with specific needs: the illiterates, the unnamed masses, the alcoholics, the divorcees, the addicts. In turn, committed Christians are trained to minister to people of a particular target group. A tremendous challenge is extended to Christian laymen out of such a program. The necessity of an in-depth study of people with particular problems and how to reach them with the good news calls for the best in thought, action, and sensitivity.

Evangelism with a New Spontaneity

Jesus said, "He that goes on trusting me, out of his inmost being shall flow rivers of living water." Jesus paints a picture of an overflowing life. I hear it partially as a reference to spontaneous sharing as we become willing channels of God's redemptive love.

Some time ago Leighton Ford of the Billy Graham Evangelistic Association, called a number of evangelical ministers who serve in

New York City. In response to the question "To what would you assign priority," there was agreement among all that "Christians are depressed and need to recover confidence in their Lord and radiance in their lives." Perhaps this is not only characteristic of New York City Christians. Maybe its coverage is far more extensive than we like to think.

Evangelism from the overflow will not be characteristic of a life which has lost its radiance. Perhaps some of our problems in motivating people have been our failures to realize this. You can't pump water from a dry well. But you can't keep the water in an artesian well from flowing. Jesus would have us to be "artesian well" Christians, who know that within is a well of water springing up into everlasting life. He would have us to become channels through whom this well overflows with rivers of living water.

I have observed in almost every church where I have the opportunity of preaching, that there are some in the group who seem to be extremely excited about what is going on. They reflect a kind of joy and radiance which is not characteristic of most members. Inevitably, I find that these "Christians who beam" have had some kind of deepening experience with God which has taken them out of the realm of the ordinary. I also observe that a large percentage of them had this deepening experience in a Lay Renewal Weekend or a Lay Witness Mission. They have taken a "journey inward," have had the deepening experience, and now are spontaneously sharing what they have discovered about what God can mean and can do in a life. Loving others seems to come easy for them, and God is real in their lives. It has helped crystalize the conviction in me that in evangelism, most of us will never go farther until we go deeper. As we go deeper, evangelism or sharing will have a tendency to become a part of our overall life-style.

When the leaders of the church in Jerusalem were questioned in court as to why they kept on telling their world about Jesus, they answered: "We cannot but speak the things we have seen and heard." This is another way of saying, "We share because we just can't help it." It was out of an overflow which couldn't be contained that they told the story. Perhaps we are moving toward this in our "new evangelism."

Evangelism with a New Simplicity

Do you ever watch the weather report on television? After several seasons of doing it, I am about to begin to grasp most of what is being said by the meteorologist. But I recall how he frequently "shot over my head" in some of those early sessions. All I wanted to know was what is going to happen weather-wise in my own area. Perhaps my family and I were planning a picnic for tomorrow afternoon. I tuned in the weather to see if the weatherman would be friend or foe in his forecast. I would see first a satellite shot of the cloud cover of planet earth superimposed over an outline of the forty-eight states. About the time I had located my state, I would learn that there was an occluded front extending along and forty miles each side of a line from Denver to El Paso. Then I would be told that there was a threatening area of cumulo nimbus clouds over Northern Illinois, and this storm system was being compounded by a low pressure system over Lake Michigan and high barometric pressure in Michigan. But what I wanted to know is, can we expect decent weather for our picnic in Fort Worth tomorrow? Sooner or later if I persevered, I would get my answer. But not until I had been taken through, what to me, was a course in advanced meteorology.

I am afraid some of our so-called evangelism has been like this. We may have wanted to show off our theological vocabulary, and we dressed the gospel up in words an advanced theological student would have difficulty understanding. Or we probably veiled the gospel by our enthusiasm for our church, Sunday School class, or pastor. Either way we failed to communicate the fact that Jesus is alive and wants to help people where they are hurting and that he has the power to make all things new in any life.

Recently I was with a friend who is pastor of one of the most strategic churches in our nation. He was terrifically excited about what's happening in his church. Out of a school on evangelism held in his church a few weeks before had come seventy-five people who were going out weekly to share the good news. The significant thing about it was that they were not going to homes to invite people to church or to brag about their pastor. When they are met at the door they immediately explain, "We have come to share with you about Jesus and what he wants to do for you." This is their simple approach. When they gain entrance, they read a simple pamphlet with the person they are visiting. They invite the person to respond to Jesus in repentance and faith. They have been seeing an average of five people trust Jesus weekly. It may sound too simple, but it is very close to the kind of evangelism one reads about in a book called Acts.

We would be wrong to refer to the gospel as "simple." The facts of the gospel are so profound that the most advanced thinking of modern man cannot plumb their depths. But we must state these facts simply, making clear the essential conditions by which one responds savingly to Jesus. This I see as a mark of the new evangelism.

Evangelism with New Flexibility

One of the most encouraging things about the "new" in evangelism is an increased flexibility. The Spirit of our text, "I am made all things to all men, that I might by all means save some," demands that evangelism be flexible in method. The willingness to change, innovate, to be pliable has characterized evangelism in recent months.

For years, almost all churches of major denominations would have nothing to do with church bus evangelism. We looked at churches which used buses as being in the "one of those" category. But how the picture has shifted. Today, over five thousand Southern Baptist churches are engaged in bus evangelism to some degree.

Many of us can recall when the guitar or other open-stringed instruments were frowned on for use in the "sanctuary." But we discovered that young people could be attracted by stringed instruments and by evangelistic musicals which employed them. Most churches have been willing to bend in this direction, and the salvation of many a young person has been the result.

In the 1960's in the thinking of many people, there was considerable tension between evangelism and social ministries. This became so pronounced that it turned into an either-or proposition for some. Polarization was endangering a balanced ministry in many congregations. But representatives of the "poles" began to listen to each other. Soon multitudes of people were realizing that instead of conflicting with each other, these two ministries complement each other. This is borne out by the fact that the Christian Social Ministries Department of the Home Mission Board of the Southern Baptist Convention has witnessed the conversion of almost fifteen thousand people in the last three years.

Openness to the "news," without automatic rejection of everything we have done in the past, must continue to characterize evangelism if any degree of effectiveness is to be maintained. We must be willing to "hang loose" as far as our thinking about methods is concerned.

This to me is the new evangelism. It represents the blowing of new winds of the Spirit. It is attempting to gear up to a twentieth-century space, electronic age. It is determined to remain anchored to a first-century message and objectives.

The new evangelism ought to offer new and better ways of telling fragmented humanity about wholeness of life in Christ. If it gets away from this, we are in perilous waters with storm signals all around us. In the book *The Christian Persuader*, the story is told of a missionary conference in the middle East where strategy was the subject of discussion. Finally the pioneer missionary in Persia, Dr. Van Ness, arose and said: "Brethren, I am sure this talk of strategy is very good. But really we have only one strategy—telling people about Jesus." The new evangelism seems to be keeping this pertinent fact well in focus!

6

Recipe for Continued Renewal

Tom Brandon

FIRST BAPTIST CHURCH,
SHERMAN, TEXAS

Lay renewal weekends bring wonderful results in the lives of laymen. In my own church, I saw Christians revived in startling ways. There was excitement, enthusiasm, love for God and fellow Christians. Many renewed their commitment to God. Some rededicated their lives afresh. One person said, "God touched me; I'll never be the same." Another reported, "It was Christ's time to make me the spiritual leader in my home." Still another said, "This weekend has meant more to me than many revivals because it gave me a chance to participate. God became very real to me and I received love, joy, and a real peace." We were on the mountaintop. We wanted to stay there.

The question my people asked was, "What is the recipe for continual renewal?" The answer is a disciplined life. Discipline is a tough business—much tougher than abstinence, which we would prefer for simplicity's sake.[1]

Nevertheless, God's word says that a disciplined life is important. First Peter 4:7 states: "The end of all things is at hand: be ye therefore sober, and watch unto prayer." Substitute "discipline" for the word "sober" and you see that life is to be disciplined. In fact, the whole passage is describing a disciplined life versus an undisciplined one. As the life of Jesus Christ was disciplined, so are we to arm ourselves with the same mind (1 Pet. 4:1). Romans 12:3 says, "Think soberly," that is, the Christian's life is to be controlled by disciplined thoughts.

In Titus, chapters one and two, the disciplined life is described as involving all ages. Pastors and spiritual leaders have a special responsibility to be disciplined (Titus 1:8). Aged men and women (Titus 2:2,4) as well as young people (Titus 2:5,6) are called to disciplined living. Every area of our lives—attitudes, thoughts, words, actions, habits—is under the call to the mind of Christ (Titus 2:12).

The question is, how disciplined are you? What does it mean and how important is it to be disciplined as Christians?

Marks of a Disciplined Life

Jesus identifies for us the disciplined life in Luke 9:23: "And he said to them all, If any man will come after me, let him deny himself, and take up his cross daily, and follow me." Four words describe the disciplined life of renewal.

Denial—A disciplined Christian is one who lives a life of denial, as seen in the statement, "let him deny himself." To deny is to disregard one's interests, to renounce, to refuse to acknowledge, to disown. The word "deny" is the same word used to describe Simon Peter's attitude toward Jesus on the night of his betrayal and trial. He refused to acknowledge Jesus, of having any relationship with him. The point is that we are to refuse to acknowledge self. We are to disregard and renounce a self-centered life.

To deny self is not just denying ourselves certain things in life; it is to deny *the self* that desires them. It is not just recognizing sins in our lives, it is acknowledging sin, which is the cause of all sins. Sin is the root, sins are the fruit or the consequences. Sin is claiming that I am the "boss" and not Christ. So to deny self is to renounce my plans, my control. It is to refuse to acknowledge self as the authority in my life. There can be no disciplined life in Christ without this firm denial of self.

Death—The mark of death is identified in the words "take up his cross." The cross means death. When we think of the cross we think of Christ's actual physical death. The cross also speaks of his death to any claims he might have had for himself. He died to them. Philippians 2:5-8 states the steps involved in his death. He made himself of no reputation, took upon himself the form of a servant, and was made in the likeness of men. In that state he humbled himself and became obedient unto death, even the death of the cross. We are to have this mind in us, "Let this mind be in you, which was also in Christ Jesus" (Phil. 2:5).

The "cross" means not only Christ's death but our death also.

The one coming after Jesus takes up *his* cross. As believers in Jesus Christ, the cross is already an accomplished fact in our lives. Galatians 2:20 says, "I have been crucified with Christ; and it is no longer I who live, but Christ lives in me; and the life which I now live in the flesh I live by faith in the Son of God, who loved me, and delivered Himself up for me" (NASB). When Christ died, we died potentially with him. At the moment we received Christ into our lives, our death with him was actually affected in us. It was a death to self and to the old nature. The "I" no longer lives, but "Christ" lives in the believer.

How is this accomplished fact made a present living reality? By consenting to this, death already died. Where? In my mind (attitudes, thoughts), emotions (responses, expectations), will (purposes, directions, decisions), and my body (outward behavior). We consent to die to our self-nature and to allow Christ to control our lives, to transform our thoughts, to redirect our wills, and to refocus our emotions. This death is effected in our lives through the ministry of the Holy Spirit (Rom. 8:13). Have you ever known that you as a believer are already dead with Christ? If you have known it, have you ever consented to it in your life? Nothing short of true and open consent to death with Christ will bring victory in Christ. You must die to yourself! There is no truly disciplined life that is not dead with Christ.

Daily—How disciplined are we to be? On Sunday morning at 11:00 o'clock, in Sunday School, in a Bible study, on a youth retreat? Jesus says we are to die *daily*. Every day we are to live the crucified life. In fact we get up every morning to die! We consent to death every day in every area of our lives. Paul says in 1 Corinthians 15:31, "I die daily."

How much of our thought life is to be under Christ's authority? The answer is found in 2 Corinthians 10:4-5, where it says: "(For the weapons of our warfare are not carnal, but mighty through God to the pulling down of strong holds;) casting down imaginations, and every high thing that exalteth itself against the knowledge of God, and bringing into captivity *every thought* to the obedience of Christ" (italics added). Every thought is to be submitted to the lordship of Jesus Christ. This is real discipline!

Is it possible to submit every thought to Christ? The answer is yes or God's Word would not have called attention to it. We do so by giving God every thought that we know is not pleasing to him. Such provides for us an opportunity for a thankful prayer to him. When this is done verbally, but quietly, he receives it and it becomes subject to Christ's lordship. In the process we need no longer struggle with it, but live in the freedom and joy of one yielded to Christ and to his Spirit.

The disciplined life is a continual relationship with Christ involving every area of our being.

Devotion—The fourth mark of a disciplined life is derived from the words, "Follow me." It is not enough to consent to death with Christ daily, we must also *crown* Jesus Christ Lord of our lives. We must consent to his resurrection life in us. As Galatians 2:20 says, "Christ lives in me" Jesus Christ is not only alive by the resurrection, but he is alive *in* the believer. As such, he is totally adequate for our inadequacies, but I must consent to his life.

There is more, as Ephesians 2:6 says. He has "made us sit together in heavenly places in Christ Jesus." Where is the believer now? He is "in Christ Jesus." The Christian is identified with Christ by union to him. He is "in heavenly places," a phrase describing not a future heaven but a spiritual relationship now. Wherever Christ is, that's where the believer is. Ephesians 1:19-23 indicates that he is at the right hand of the Father in heavenly places. He is in the position of authority that the Father has given to him and, therefore, all things are under him. By virtue of the believer's union with Christ we have been delegated this authority by which we live, pray, and witness. It is both an awesome privilege and responsibility given to us by grace through faith. This relationship also must be acknowledged and entered into by consent. When we give that consent, we experience his power and authority in us. We are thus enabled to live the disciplined life. We live by his authority in us and, therefore, have a new boldness to live a disciplined life.

If you are living a disciplined life, these four marks will ring true in your life. If you are not living the disciplined life, you can. How is this possible? First, confess to God that self has been in control and not God. Second, consent to death with Christ, not by feeling, but by faith. Third, commit your life to die daily to self. Fourth, crown Jesus Christ Lord right now as an act of your will. As you take these steps your daily relationship with Jesus Christ will grow and there will be an ever-deepening joy and power in your life.

There is something else that is necessary if we are to live a disciplined life.

Musts of a Disciplined Life

Once you have yielded yourself to Christ and are daily practicing that relationship, there are two things that will enable the Holy Spirit to make this real and exciting to you. These two basic essentials are stated in Acts 6:4. This passage indicates that the apostles led the church to solve a problem of fellowship. They not only brought peace to the fellowship, but they also stated some basic priorities for disciplined lives. That to which they committed themselves became the priorities of their fellow-believers, and they, in turn, become our priorities by which to live. They said, "But we will give ourselves *continually* to prayer, and to the ministry of the Word." Here are the two "musts" of a disciplined life: prayer and the Word of God.

First, there must be continual prayer in our lives. Many times the Bible tells us to pray. Jesus taught a parable "That men ought always to pray, and not to faint" (Luke 18:1). We are told to "continue instant in prayer" (Rom. 12:12). This means to be devoted to prayer and ever persistent in it. Paul teaches us that the warfare of a Christian is prayer. In Ephesians 6:10-17, he describes the enemy and the equipment of a Christian soldier. Then he states how the soldier is to wage warfare by the spiritual exercise of prayer. Verse 18 says, "Praying always with all prayer and supplication in the Spirit, and watching thereunto with all perseverance and supplication for all saints." Unquestionably, prayer is essential.

Dr. J. H. Jowett said, "I'd rather teach one man to pray than ten men to preach." "What is the secret of revival?" a great evangelist was asked. He replied: "There is no secret. Revival always comes in answer to prayer." How many get alone with God in prayer and Bible study? In a survey of five hundred theological students, it was revealed that 93 percent did not have a devotional life.

In West Africa years ago, it was the custom of Christians to leave their huts to go into the forest each day for prayer with God. Each made his own path. If his path grew up in weeds, it was a sign that prayer had been neglected, and one brother would say to another, "Is the grass growing on your path, brother?" Prayer is essential to a disciplined life.

Second, we must give ourselves continually to the ministry of God's Word. What place does the Word of God have in your life? Without it you are defenseless and open to attacks from the enemies of a disciplined life. With it you have "the sword of the Spirit" (Eph. 6:17), a spiritual weapon that is "quick and powerful and sharper than any twoedged sword" (Heb. 4:12).

The book of Acts is a living illustration that the word of God is powerful. Acts 19:20 summarizes the effectiveness of God's word in the New Testament days when it says, "So mightily grew the word of God and prevailed." In fact, the mighty movements of God have been associated with the word of God.

Moreover, any success we experience in the Christian life will be related in degree to our commitment to God's Word. This was the key to Joshua's success: "This book of the law shall not depart out of thy mouth; but thou shalt meditate therein day and night, that thou mayest observe to do according to all that is written therein: for then thou shalt have good success" (Josh. 1:8). This is our secret, too.

Open your heart to God's Word. Desire it as food (1 Pet. 2:2). Hunger and thirst for it as your way of life (Matt. 5:6). Get into God's Word! Memorize it to store it in your heart; visualize it as the way of truth by which you are to live; and personalize it by praying it back to God. When you do, you are meditating on God's

Word, and your life will be filled and changed by it.

There are two practical suggestions to be made about these two disciplines in our lives. One, the morning is a special time with the heavenly Father. Take time to be with him in the mornings. Psalm 5:3 says, "In the morning will I direct my prayer." Exodus 16:7 says, "And in the morning, then ye shall see the glory of the Lord." This is not the only time, to be sure, but it is the freshest time to be with him.

Second, there are three words that must become real to us if we are to be strong in prayer and the Word of God. They are found in Proverbs 20:13, "*Love not sleep,* lest you come to poverty (italics added)." Be careful or sleep will rob you of spiritual blessings.

Conclusion

God is waiting to fill our lives with freedom, power, and boldness. Such comes, not by tying things on to our lives, but by being transformed by a new relationship with Jesus Christ in death and life. This relationship results in an overflow of our lives in the daily disciplines or prayer and God's Word. It is futile and frustrating to approach a disciplined life otherwise. The fullness of Christ's life awaits your response to his steps.

Notes

[1] David Haney, *The Idea of the Laity,* (Grand Rapids: Zondervan, 1973), p. 78.

7

The Total Dimension of Renewal

William Pinson, Jr.

SOUTHWESTERN BAPTIST THEOLOGICAL SEMINARY,
FORT WORTH, TEXAS

Renewal means wholeness, coming alive to the total gospel. It is for all Christians, not just for clergy or "holy people." The new life is to affect not only churches, but also families, businesses, labor unions, schools, and neighborhoods. Renewal is to affect morality as well as devotional life, ethics as well as evangelism, ministry as well as worship. There is a necessary link between morality and revival. The Bible indicates when people turn from their wicked ways as well as pray, God will heal their land (2 Chron. 7:14); that God will not respond to the prayers of those whose hands are soiled by immoral deeds until they cease their evil ways (Isa. 1:15-17); that the prayers of *righteous* men avail much (Jas. 5:16). Similarly, evangelism is related to new life and social reform. Conversion results in a life of good works and ministry (Eph. 2:8-10).

Renewal is rooted in the biblical truth that God is concerned about life, not merely religion and that he desires the transformation of persons, not just the salvation of souls. Because the Bible is concerned about how saved persons are to live as well as how persons are to be saved, our concern must be this broad too. All of life is the domain of renewal in Christ. Jesus issued marching orders that stressed wholeness: "*All* power is given unto me . . . teach *all* nations . . . to observe *all* things whatsoever I have commanded you . . . I am with you *alway*" (Matt. 28:18-20, italics added). The wholeness of renewal is based on the entire Bible. It includes all people and total human need. It is concerned with the total dimensions of a church.

All the Bible

Different persons in the renewal movement are attracted to different emphases. One stresses the role of the laity, the fact that all in Christ are called to be ministers. Others point up key pietistic

53

themes such as prayer, meditation, and Bible study. Many spring to attention when the Spirit-filled life is mentioned. Others come alive to evangelism or ministry or Christian social concern. Spiritual gifts hold a special allure for many. Highlighting particular emphases is not bad unless a person is blind to equally important biblical themes.

The Bible is our guide for renewal. To speak of the Bible as the Word of God is common among Baptists. A hallmark of our faith has been an emphasis on the Bible as God's inspired written Word. Anyone among us suggesting that a portion of the Scripture is not true, trustworthy, or important had better be prepared for serious consequences. We profess to believe the whole Bible. But do we? Could it be that some who rush to *defend* the truth of the whole Bible fail to *share* the truth of the whole Bible? Is it possible that some deny portions of the Word of God by never preaching, teaching, singing, or discussing them? The Word of God is sharper than a two-edged sword, but do we sometimes render the Bible a dull, single-edged blade?

Let us be a people of the Book—of the whole Book. At great cost God inspired and preserved the Bible. He expects us to share all of it. We are not to rummage through the Scriptures picking texts here and there which fit our theological fancy and discarding the rest. To deal exclusively with the social concerns texts and ignore those on evangelism misrepresents the Scriptures. However, to stress only those parts which deal with evangelism and skip the others for all practical purposes undermines belief in the inspiration of the whole Bible.

Stress the total Bible. Share "If a man has means and sees his brother in need, yet closes his heart against his brother, how can he claim that he has love for God in his heart?" (1 John 3:17) as well as "Ye must be born again" (John 3:7). Share "Whosoever will call on the name of the Lord will be saved" (Rom. 10:13) and "If a man says he loves God and hates his brother, he is a liar" (1 John 4:20). Share "Love your neighbor as yourself" (Matt. 22:39, RSV) and "Believe on the Lord Jesus Christ and you will be saved" (Acts 16:32, RSV). Share "God is no respector of persons" (Acts

10:34) as well as "The wages of sin is death; but the gift of God is eternal life through Jesus Christ our Lord" (Rom. 6:23).

Responding to God's total revealed Word is an awesome responsibility. In order to ease the task we are sometimes tempted to cut out portions. However, Christians have been commissioned to proclaim the Word not to prune it. The New Testament ends with a solemn warning to those who would dare cut out any part of God's Word: "And if any man shall take away from the words of the book of this prophecy, God shall take away his part out of the book of life" (Rev. 22:19). The threat may be related only to the book of Revelation, but it certainly applies to all of God's Word.

Total Human Need

With the whole Bible as our guide, Christians need to be concerned about all aspects of human life—spiritual, physical, mental, emotional, social. Those finding new life in Christ should be concerned about people who are kept out of Baptist churches because of race and class as we have been about those let in without benefit of Baptist immersion. We need to become as concerned about what the poor have for supper as we have been about who is eligible to partake of the Lord's Supper. If we share the whole Bible, we will deal with repentance and racism, faith and family, regeneration and revolution, justification and justice, sanctification and sex, hell and housing, heaven and honesty, salvation and starvation—because the Bible speaks to all of these. Renewal, when based on the Bible, will result in moral and ethical renewal.

Recognizing that God is the creator, the renewed Christian will practice good stewardship toward his creation. Christians are accountable for the pollution, the dirty air and water, and the littered earth. The boast of the "self-made man" is blasphemy for it is God who gives the power to get wealth. The defiant cry, "It's mine, I'll do with it what I want," is a denial of the biblical truth that everything belongs to God. Any economy—socialist, communist, or capitalist—that plunders the earth, uses natural resources to make fortunes for a few, brings suffering to the many, and fouls the environment stands under the judgment of God.

Renewal calls for action that deals with social problems and conditions that are ungodly.

Up until recently many churches and individual Christians did little to try to counter evil social forces. Now we are at least talking about dealing with the problems. Many are realizing the Bible clearly indicates God cares about the whole man and about all aspects of human life. He is concerned about economics, politics, and family as well as worship, evangelism, small groups, and missions. God calls his people to minister to human need and to work to alter the social conditions of men as well as to preach the gospel. Actually, God does not so much give us an answer to how we can have a better future as he makes us answer. We are not so much called upon to *give answers* as we are challenged to *be an answer.*

As the people of God, using the minds which God has given us and the tools which he has placed in our hands, we are to work to root out evil and to establish good in our society. We must repudiate the modernism which declares that we are "to preach the gospel and save souls, nothing else" and get back to the biblical message which declares, "Go into all the world," "Faith without works is dead," "By their fruits ye shall know them."

The great churchmen have sided with the poor, lashed out against injustice, called for reform of prisons, pled the cause of the orphan, condemned racism, and clearly proclaimed that Jesus must be lord. *John Wesley* rode the length and breadth of England crying, "Ye must be born again." He also condemned the slave trade, blasted the alcohol industry, and ministered to the poor. *Charles Finney* set revival fires burning throughout America. At the same time he delivered the most blistering attacks upon slavery uttered in his time. *Charles Spurgeon* stood Sunday after Sunday as the best-known Baptist preacher in the world declaring salvation through faith in Jesus Christ. He also encouraged his church to build orphanages, schools for the poor, homes for the aged, soup kitchens for the hungry, and publishing houses for decent literature. He himself condemned child labor, racism, and the exploitation of the poor. No one pled with people more earnestly than *George W. Truett* to come to Christ. He also called Christians to their responsibility on social issues. For example, from the steps of the Capitol in Washington he not only set forth the cause of religious liberty but also urged the United States to back the League of Nations. In our own day, *Billy Graham* is eloquent in his testimony that there is no conflict between missions and ministry, evangelism and social action. Renewal is the discovery of the greatness of our heritage.

The renewed person must ask, "What can I do? What can I as one individual or even one local church do to alter social conditions?" Probably not very much. You alone can't transform the world. You alone can't change the course of your nation. Alone you can really do little more than transform your home, improve your neighborhood, and stimulate your church. Enough people, however, acting as individuals in this way would alter the course of the world. That is much of what renewal is about.

The point is to think small. Too often we ponder grandiose schemes while walking past immediate opportunities we could do something about. For example, you could work to clear up some of the inconsistencies which exist in so many personal lives. How many do you know who spend huge sums of money to kill weeds and bugs in their well-kept yards but refuse to support programs to kill rats that bite babies in their cribs in slums? How many do you know who hire Negroes to work in their homes and care for their children in church nurseries but protest when Negroes try to move next door to them or want to join their church? How many do you know who cry over a dent in the fender of their new car but calmly read about the slaughter of helpless men, women, and children in foreign wars? How many do you know who howl about "crime in the streets" when it involves demonstrations but who only grumble when "crime in the streets" involves drunken or wreckless driving—which by the way, accounts for more deaths and destruction than all the riots and demonstrations put together? Renewal calls for transformation of our attitudes, values, and character.

Renewal also calls for new life in family, daily work, and citizenship. Again the Bible serves as the guide for how Christians are to live in these basic orders of society. Integrity, responsibility, courage, honesty, love, concern—these are some of the words which describe the biblical ideal for the Christian as family member, workman, and citizen. By improving the quality of family life, daily work, and government a Christian helps renew society according to God's plan.

The renewal movement, of course, won't bring in a perfect world. It won't make us perfect individuals either. Only Christ's coming again will usher in the new heaven and the new earth and eliminate social evils. In the meantime, we have a responsibility to live godly lives in Christ Jesus, to work for justice, to combat evil. By so conducting ourselves we prepare for his coming.

Whole Churches

Renewal, if effective, will transform churches. Of all institutions, churches ought to be most affected by renewal. Some renewal enthusiasts have given up on local churches and majored on small groups, personal pietism, and retreat centers. Yet the local church remains the chief organized method by which God works in the world. Renewal efforts ought to major on churches and should have an impact on all aspects of a church's life and program.

Churches are often criticized for being irrelevant. Some may be. Yet when a church is true to its mission, it is the most relevant institution in the world. No other organization is devoted to both the temporal and eternal aspects of humankind. Renewal must not pass the churches by. Rather we must come alive again to what God wants his churches to be and do.

The body of Christ is to function as Christ did during his earthly ministry. Jesus ministered to persons by word and deed. Proclamation and ministry are both essential. They go together. No church can be as evangelistic as it ought to be until it is involved in programs of ministry and social action. Many of Jesus' preaching opportunities came because he healed sick bodies and challenged sick social conditions. The people wanted to hear what he had to say because his actions showed he cared for them. He did not go around putting up posters reading "Come hear Jesus of Nazareth preach on the mountain." Rather he "went about doing good" and the people flocked to hear him gladly. Shouldn't this be our pattern, too? Great churches have never been confined to honeycombs of classrooms for education nor barns for preaching. They have been involved in ministry to total human need as Christ was. Renewal will result in such ministry and such ministry will stimulate renewal.

The spirit of fellowship within a church is also important. The preaching and teaching of the Word call persons to love God and one another. Jesus told his disciples, "By this shall all men know that ye are my disciples, if ye have love one to another" (John 13:35). People who love one another care and pray for each other. Such closeness in the early church caused outsiders to exclaim, "Look how much they love one another!" I wonder what the outside world says about us? Part of our witness is our fellowship. Warm, loving Christian fellowship will draw people to our churches and to our Christ. We need a renewal of fellowship.

Renewal must result in church involvement in Christian social action and ministry. Some people are calling for a cutback in church activity. However, effective churches are not eliminating but rather adding meaningful activity. Churches are undertaking ministries to a wide variety of persons. Special programs are in operation for the aging, young, unwed parents, mentally ill, physically handicapped, retarded, shut-in, sick, prisoner, delinquent, poor, international, addict, alcoholic, released offender, runaway youth, nonreader, and others. Ministries include medical clinics, clothes and food centers, tutoring, job training and placement, halfway houses, counseling centers, home Bible study, telephone counseling, homemaking classes, apartment house ministry, literacy training, and citizenship classes.

A number of churches are realizing the need for social action as well as personal ministry. They see that it is not enough to tutor the slow learner without also doing something about the social circumstances which caused him to be mentally deficient. They understand that it is not enough to provide clothes and food to the poor and do nothing about the near starvation wages many are paid. Numerous action groups are being formed by churches to tackle social problems.

Churches are also learning that they alone cannot handle the challenge of ministry in the modern world. Social issues as well as personal need call for corporate action. In rural America, problems were normally handled by individuals or small groups. Sewage disposal consisted of building an outhouse. Air pollution was solved by telling your neighbor not to burn wet trash downwind. In today's urban, technological America such problems call for group action. If people are to be cared for, churches must learn to express Christian love through social action. In our world we cannot love adequately unless we love corporately as well as personally.

All church programs will be shallow humanism unless they communicate the good news of Christ. Part of the struggle of today's church is how to effectively communicate the gospel. In sharing the Christian faith, we must remember that in some cases our only ministry may be to declare the eternal hope in Jesus Christ. For many there are no temporal solutions to their problems. Change will not come soon enough for millions now alive to eliminate their suffering. Without lessening Christian social action or reducing the gospel to promises of pie in the sky by and by, we must not be ashamed to tell the suffering masses of our world about a city where God will wipe away all tears from their eyes and there will be no more grief, crying, or pain.

Renewal means new approaches in church programming to meet total human need, personal and social, ethical and spiritual, moral and devotional. There is no orthodoxy of methodology. Any method of sharing that is in keeping with the Bible is acceptable. What works for one church will not work for another. Diversity of life-style calls for increased tolerance among Baptists. God opens new doors every morning and we must have the courage to work through them. We should experiment with new approaches and methods. This does not mean abandoning old methods simply because they are old. The test is not, "Is it old or new?" but "Does it serve to effectively carry out the mission of the church?"

Baptists traditionally have been nontraditional. We have been willing to open new streets in the city of God. We were lumped with the radical wing of the Reformation for good reason. We were regarded with suspicion by the monarchies of Europe because we favored new forms of government. The established churches of America showed us ill will because we proposed new church structures. Baptists spread across the frontier like a prairie fire because we abandoned traditional methods of establishing churches and training ministers. Other Baptists regarded Southern Baptists as radical and unorthodox when we adopted a board and convention approach to denominationalism. Is the Baptist genius for developing creative, innovative, and effective approaches of Christian ministry still alive? Yes! And renewal can fan a spark into a flame of creativity.

Conclusion

What if we fail to respond to the new life God is endeavoring to pump into us? What if we go on with business as usual? What if we bow down in doctrinal or institutional feuds? What if we soft-pedal portions of the Bible in order to attract new members? Perhaps God will raise up another people to do what we would not do. He may let the inevitable wages of our sin be paid—death. Death in our cities as pollution, prejudice, riot take their toll; death of little children through hunger, rat bite, drugs, and violence; death of our churches as they perish from neglect, racism, inflexibility, and the shame of failure to meet the challenges around them; death of our freedom and democracy as revolutionaries capitalize on the intolerable situation created by our apathy; death eternal to the multitudes who never clearly hear or see our witness unto Jesus Christ.

This need not be! Let us participate in life, the abundant life Jesus came to give. Let us share that life which affects all of us and all of our relationships. Let us share in all kinds of ways through our churches as the Holy Spirit empowers us. Then renewal will transform individuals, families, businesses, schools, governments, communities, as well as churches. Certainly we must have priorities. We can't deal with everything all the time. Majoring on minor issues and going off on tangents are irresponsible. We should concentrate on the central emphasis of the written and incarnate Word—how lost men can be saved and how saved men ought to live. In so acting we can write new chapters in the story of God's people—bold, courageous, expansive chapters. More important we can honor God and bring life to millions.

8

The Power Life

James Mahoney

FULL-TIME EVANGELIST
NACOGDOCHES, TEXAS

Elijah was a prophet of enormous power. The Scriptures record eleven remarkable miracles that were attributed to his ministry. From the first day he suddenly burst upon the scene to prophesy a three-year drought, his entire life and service was characterized by power. Elijah could pray down fire or water, whatever was needed at the time. Elijah had never experienced anything more dramatic and demonstrative than his last prophecy in which he announced God was going to sweep him off the earth in a whirlwind! None of his miraculous experiences were more significant than this last one, because the exit of Elijah in a blaze of glory forever answers a question of vital importance: *"Can the power of God be passed on from one generation to the next?"* Must a generation ever settle for merely sitting around and talking about "old-time" power . . . or is there *new power* available to replace the old? Can God's power be passed on as a spiritual legacy?

That question was forever settled in our text. Seemingly out of nowhere, a large whirlwind blew through and swept Elijah off the earth, his mantle dropping to the ground! Elisha, the successor of Elijah, instantly stepped forward, picked up Elijah's mantle, and called down heaven's power. (A mantle was the cloak of a prophet which identified him as a man of godly authority and power.)

What a stupendous discovery—to know the power of God is forever available; that is, the power of God is available for any person who comes to God with *Elisha's qualifications.*

A careful study of our text reveals at least three things which qualified Elisha as a recipient of Elijah's power. We can appropriate power for any new day if we possess these same three characteristics.

When We Are Weak

We can appropriate God's power *when we are weak.* After having witnessed Elijah's mighty deeds, Elisha became quite conscious of his own inadequacy. It is obvious that Elisha appeared somewhat inferior when compared with Elijah, for the young prophets of Bethel and Jericho rather condescendingly questioned his knowledge of Elijah's predicted departure: "There the young prophets of Bethel Seminary came out to meet them and asked Elisha, 'Did you know that the Lord is going to take Elijah away from you today?' " (v. 3, TLB). Elisha's sharp retort seems to indicate a hypersensitivity on his part and that he harbored feelings of inadequacy: " 'Quiet,' Elisha snapped, 'of course I know it' " (v. 3). Elisha's sense of inadequacy was not misplaced. He *was* inadequate. One thing was clear to Elisha. He would never be able to carry out Elijah's ministry in his own strength and ability. After all, when God called him, he was "plowing a field with eleven other teams ahead of him; he was at the end of the line with the last team" (1 Kings 19:19, TLB). He ranked eleventh in a line of eleven plowmen.

Therefore, when Elisha was asked what he most desired from God, his instant response to Elijah was: "Let a double portion of thy spirit be upon me" (2 Kings 2:9). This request for a "double portion" of Elijah's spirit was not the ambitious desire of a self-centered egotist wishing to excel his predecessor. It was an assessment of deep need by a humble man of God. Elisha considered Elijah twice the man he was, in every respect . . . *so he thought it would take twice as much of the Spirit's power if he was to continue Elijah's work.*

Mark it down. An important prerequisite for appropriating the power of God is a deep realization of how much you need it! God has a way of using those who seem incapable.

In marked contrast to Elisha's *humility,* most Christians are just too *handy.* Blind to our own inadequacy, we hurry to and fro, doing things *for* God as if everything depends upon *us.* Our attempt to lend God a hand is like a flea offering help to an elephant. The tragedy is that we have millions of American Christians serving in thousands of churches with little or no effect upon our nation because we have never realized our need of a power beyond ourselves for accomplishing God's work.

One would think we would have learned better by now, for this was one of the first lessons God tried to teach mankind.

God has always expected service from his children. One of the reasons God delivered the Israelites from their slavery in Egypt was that they might more freely *serve* him. God stated this several times: "Let my people go, that they may serve me" (Ex. 7:16; 8:20; 9:1; 9:13).

Even after their deliverance, the Israelites failed miserably in their service to God. *Typically, they were just too handy.* The Bible says they "rejoiced in the works of their own *hands*" (Acts 7:41, italics added). In the incident to which this verse refers, Israel rejected their leader and set about to make an image of worship by their own doing (Ex. 32:1-9). They did not really need God (so they thought), and they set about to establish their own righteousness and erected an altar . . . to and for themselves. But God was not in it. In fact, God destroyed it (Ex. 32:20). They were just too handy!

Interestingly enough, Moses failed once to deliver Israel because of the same problem—he was just too handy: "He supposed . . . that God *by his hand* would deliver them" (Acts 7:25, italics added). Though an Israelite, Moses had been reared within the palace of Egypt. He was quite outstanding. The Bible said he was "learned in all the wisdom of the Egyptians and was mighty in words and in deeds" (Acts 7:22). One day he set out to deliver the Israelites from their bondage. He came upon an Egyptian who was mistreating an Israelite. To avenge the Israelite, Moses killed and buried the Egyptian. Strong winds blew the sand away from the grave. The body was uncovered; his deed was discovered; and he fled for his life. Moses tried to lead Israel by his own ability, but the Israelites *rejected* him (Ex. 2:15). Moses fled.

However, forty years later God *did* call Moses to lead Israel out of Egypt: "This Moses whom they refused, saying, Who made thee a ruler . . . the same did God send to be a ruler and a deliver" (Acts 7:35). Moses was a changed man. He was not so handy now.

God found him on the "backside of the desert." When God called him to lead Israel he was very reluctant to accept saying, "Who am I, that I should go?" (Ex. 3:11). Quite a difference in this Moses from the presumptuous young man who swaggered out of a palace to help God forty years before. Perhaps the reticence of Moses was most vividly focused when he reminded God of Israel's former unwillingness to follow him and asked what *authority* he would have. God's answer was superb. God asked, "What is that in thine hand?" (Ex. 4:2). Moses replied, "A rod." It was a common shepherd's rod. He was not so "handy" now. Moses had been reduced to a humble sheepherder, tending his father-in-law's flock on the backside of the desert. So all Moses had in his hand now was a common shepherd's rod, and notice, God told Moses to even throw it down: "Cast it on the ground" (Ex. 4:3). Gone is the finery of palace dress. Gone is the power of palace privilege. Gone is the princely prestige. Gone are the friends in high circles. Gone is the strong young body. Gone is the razor-sharp mind, fresh from Egyptian schooling. Gone is the zeal to avenge. Gone is the self-confidence. *And now, even his shepherd's rod must go!*

Never forget this moment. Visualize Moses as he stands empty-handed before God. Moses, as he is seen in just that instant, is the lasting image of the kind of man God uses. You must throw down every single thing in your hand. God calls the empty-handed. Surrender your self-sufficiency. When Moses threw down the rod, it became a *snake*, symbol of the satanic nature of mere human ability in God's service. You see, Satan will seldom hinder you from doing things *for* God, for that prevents God from doing things *through* you . . . and God's doings are of such greater magnitude!

Next, God told Moses to pick up the snake. Moses did, and it became a rod in his hand. But it is no longer a shepherd's rod; it had now become "the rod of God" (Ex. 4:20). Before it had been a man's rod. "It could do no more than a man could do and could strike no harder than the strength of the man whose hand held it." [1] Now the snake of self-sufficiency is out of it. Henceforth, it was referred to as the "rod of God." Moses now raises the rod in battle and the Amalekites are routed. Moses lifts it to strike a rock and water miraculously gushes forth. Moses holds the rod over the Red Sea and the waters divide allowing the Israelites to walk through on dry ground. Then the waters reconverged on Egypt's pursuing troops, to drown them. Israel is delivered from Egypt! Ian Thomas pointed out that when Moses tried to tackle the job he could not even bury one Egyptian successfully. But, "when *God* tackled the job, he buried the whole lot of them in the Red Sea." [2]

It is not *ability*, but *availability* that qualifies a man for God's service. God most fully empowers those who realize their own weakness and inadequacy. This is the sense of what the Lord told Paul, "My grace is sufficient for thee: for my strength is made perfect in weakness . . . glory in infirmities, that the power of Christ" may be yours (2 Cor. 12:9).

Several other factors are necessary to qualify for God's empowering of our lives.

Where the Action Is

We can appropriate God's power *when we stay where the action is.* One can scarcely read our text without being impressed with another very obvious attribute with regard to Elisha: he desperately wanted to be in on what God was up to. Indeed, this seems to be the sense of the entire flow of our text. On three consecutive occasions Elijah mentioned being sent by God: "The Lord hath sent me to Bethel" (2 Kings 2:2); "The Lord hath sent me to Jericho" (v. 4); "The Lord hath sent me to Jordan" (v. 6).

Furthermore, on each occasion Elijah encouraged Elisha to stay behind. Why would Elijah suggest that Elisha stay behind? Perhaps Elijah wanted to spare Elisha from possible danger. Perhaps Elijah, like the young prophets, thought Elisha was not yet ready for such an experience. In either case, Elisha was put to the *test*. His determined, repeated reply to Elijah was, "As the Lord liveth, and as thy soul liveth, I will not leave thee" (vv. 2, 4, 6).

Elisha wanted to be right in the middle of what God was doing. He did not want to miss out on anything. This seemed to be a vital ingredient in appropriating God's power. When Elisha later requested a double portion of the Spirit's power, he was told in verse 10 that his reception of that double portion was dependent upon his remaining with Elijah through everything.

Actually, Elijah is establishing an important principle: *"If you want the mantle, you have to be there when it falls."* This is to say that God's fullest power is granted to those most determined to be a part of what God is doing—those who want in on all that God is doing.

Not everyone wants in on what God is doing—not by any means. Too often the activity of God's Spirit is life-changing, almost earth-shaking, like a whirlwind. Things get all turned around in a whirlwind. Old traditions are ripped away, people's priorities are rearranged, old methods become obsolete, interests change, life-styles are transformed, behavior is altered, life-goals are reversed, attitudes are altered, loyalties are shifted, and interpersonal relationships are affected. All of which will require life adjustments on the part of those involved. The young prophets of Bethel said to Elisha: "Knowest thou that the Lord will take away thy master from thy head today?" (v. 3). Unlike the prophet Elisha, they did not want to be anywhere near Elijah when the whirlwind hit. They wanted no part of it.

Likewise, not everyone longs to experience the power of real renewal, for it comes in on winds of change. The naked truth is that *most* of us do not want to be where the action is. It is too demanding, and we are too comfortable. The motto of many churches is, "Please don't rock the boat."

Perhaps such reticence with regard to renewal is somewhat understandable. For when Christians begin to live and serve in the Spirit's power, they will draw satanic opposition like a magnet attracts metal. As Elijah said, to request the Spirit's power is to "ask a hard thing" (v. 10).

Moreover, the young prophets of Jericho also knew Elijah was about to be taken up in a whirlwind. However, contrary to those of Bethel, the young prophets of Jericho followed Elijah as far as Jordan. Then they stood back "to view afar off" (v. 7). While the prophets of Bethel did not want any part of what was happening, the prophets of Jericho wanted to stand by and watch what happened.

There will always be Christians like this. They care enough to be *inconvenienced*, but they do not really want to be *involved*. Such Christians never appropriate God's power; they get in only on what God does through others, while they stand by and watch what happens.

How many times have we watched some couple roam throughout a city, like spiritual vagabonds, in a desperate search for a church where something is "happening." Then, when they find one, they join and *sit!* They take no responsibility. They attend because this is the best show in town. Like the prophets of Jericho, they just like to see what happens.

In stark contrast, Elisha went on with Elijah to the other side of Jordan—and beyond. The Scriptures explicitly state "they two went over" (v. 8), and it was "as they still went on" (v. 11) that God's whirlwind was experienced.

So the question seems to be—how far are we willing to go in order to be a part of all God wants to do in our world? Just how much do we want God's power? How obedient are we willing to be?

Three questions can test the measure of our desire, "Will we go with him to Bethel, to Jericho, and to Jordan . . . as Elisha did?"

Will we go with him to Bethel? Bethel was a holy place at whose altar men really got right with God (Gen. 35:1-3). Likewise, in our text, when Elijah's mantle fell, Elisha *first* rent his garments (a symbolic act of contrition and purification), *then* picked up the mantle and called down God's power. We must ask ourselves this question: *Am I really willing to ask forgiveness from God and others for all I have done wrong?* Such a willingness is necessary in order to appropriate spiritual power.

Will we go with him to Jericho? The children of Israel were to march to Jericho each day, encircle it, and return, repeating this for six days. They were to march around it seven times on the seventh day (Josh. 6). They obeyed these instructions explicitly, and God's power fell. We must ask ourselves this question: *"Am I really willing to do anything God asks?"*

Will you go with him to Jordan? Jordan represents the place of *exceptional* obedience, the furthest point to be reached. The children of Israel finally experienced the power and full blessing of their promised land when they crossed over Jordan. They made it over Jordan because they were fully obedient, "And they answered Joshua, saying, All that thou commandest us we will do, and whithersoever thou sendest us, we will go" (Josh. 1:16). We must ask ourselves this question: *"Am I really willing to do everything God asks?"*

God's power is inseparably linked with his purpose. The degree of our obedience will always equal the degree of our empowering. It all depends upon just how much we are willing for God to do through us. *If we want the mantle, we must be there when it falls.* This necessitates obedience: "The Holy Spirit . . . is given by God to all that obey him" (Acts 5:32, TLB). God's power will flow through those who stay where the action is, those who burn with a desperate desire to do his will.

When We Refuse to Fake It

We can appropriate God's power *when we refuse to fake it.* Elisha was a man of integrity. He would settle for nothing but the real thing. He wanted nothing less and nothing other than Elijah's ability to appropriate the sheer power of God. When Elijah was whisked off the earth, he dropped his mantle behind. Elisha picked it up, immediately rent his clothes, and approached the river Jordan (vv. 12-13). Just hours before, Elisha had seen Elijah smite the waters with his mantle, and the waters parted for them to cross (v. 8). So, in the very same way Elisha smote the waters with the mantle and cried, *"Where is the Lord God of Elijah?"* (v. 14, italics added). The waters instantly divided, and Elisha walked through!

Elisha had too much integrity to fake it. So he strode forward to test his readiness. It was time to find out if he could appropriate God's power or not! There comes a time when we must put our lives to the test if we ever expect to serve in the power of God. We must take hold of our lives, commit ourselves for an activity of service to which God leads us, and trust God to enable us for the task!

This is exactly what many are afraid to do. We are far too spiritually insecure to put our lives to the test. We are afraid God will not answer, the power will not fall, and we will be revealed for what we really are: *hypocrites.* Busily playing our spiritual games, we pretend to be people of real prayer who really enjoy Christian service and sacrifice. We feign real love for God, and pose as if we have assurance about our relationship with him. We quickly change from one role to another, always a little fearful someone will come along and catch us with our masks down.

Modern youth have a word for unreal people—they call them *"plastic."* Ours is a day of mass-produced, "plastic" models of yesterday's hand-made originals. And "plastic" Christians we are! We launch a revival meeting, receive seventy-five new members, and call it a Pentecost. We constantly maneuver and unceasingly placate to avoid factions and division, then call it fellowship. We organize thirty-five people to visit for the purpose of inviting folks to church and call this a soul-winning program. We sew patches on quilts and call ourselves missionary. We give far less than an honest tithe and say we "support the church." If a church of two thousand members baptizes a mere one hundred converts per year, we refer to ourselves as an evangelistic church.

There is quite a difference between Elisha and most of us. We step forward and cry, "Where is the Lord God of *mediocrity?*" But Elisha cried, "Where is the Lord God of Elijah?" That is, where is the God who divides the waters and answers with fire. In most cases, if you would search for the mitigating influence behind our hesitancy to call for a demonstration of Elijah's power and the cause for much of our timidity in service, you would discover a large portion of pride. Too proud to admit our doubts and inadequacies, we "fake" spirituality, when we cannot even pray up the answer to a minor daily problem!

Oh, for some Christians who will prepare, put themselves to the test, and then with audacious faith stand amidst our modern-day mediocrity and cry out, "Where is the Lord God of Elijah!"

We can appropriate God's power *when we refuse to fake it.* So never pretend to be more powerful than you are, but keep testing your life until you see things happen which take the Holy Spirit to explain!

Conclusion

Paul S. Rees tells of a Keswick Conference in which a preacher enumerated the great blessings which came in his ministry as a consequence of Spirit-filled service.[3] Following the sermon, a young man came to the speaker and said, "I am so thirsty. I need the power of the Spirit in my life."

The preacher said, "I can take you to the place where I was filled, and anyone can be filled at that place. Would you like to come with me?"

"Yes, by all means," the young man replied.

So they walked out of the conference grounds and up a mountain. As they sauntered along, the preacher kept talking about the glory resulting from a Spirit-filled life. Once in a while the young man would come to a clearing in the woods and ask, "Is this the place?"

"No, but it isn't much farther; it's up here a little distance."

They kept walking. The preacher kept talking. The young man's thirst kept increasing.

They reached a plateau and the young man asked again, "Is this the place?"

He asked the same when they walked out into a valley, again at the edge of a clearing, and at the top of each hill.

"Is this the place?" he asked again and again. Finally, he could stand it no longer. He fell upon his knees and all but shouted, "I can't go any farther. I must pray to be filled right now!"

The preacher turned and said, *"This is the place! This is the place!"*

Do you see? When we come to the place where we want to be filled with the Spirit, that's the place where you will be filled!

Notes

[1] Jack Taylor, *The Key to Triumphant Living*, (Nashville: Broadman Press, 1971), p. 83.

[2] Ian Thomas, *The Saving Life of Christ*, (Grand Rapids: Zondervan, 1968), p. 65.

[3] This section quoted from my book, *Journey into Fullness*, (Nashville: Broadman Press, 1974), p. 59.

9

An Exciting Journey

Reid Hardin

HOME MISSION BOARD, SOUTHERN BAPTIST CONVENTION,
ATLANTA, GEORGIA

"Come, let us return to the Lord; it is he who has torn us—he will heal us. He has wounded—he will bind us up. In just a couple of days, or three at the most, he will set us on our feet again, to live in his kindness! Oh, that we might know the Lord! Let us press on to know him, and he will respond to us as surely as the coming of dawn or the rain or early spring" (Hos. 6:1-3, TLB).

Thousands of lay people and clergy are reporting that these words of Hosea are being fulfilled in them. God is working in their lives to set them on their feet again. They are experiencing the renewing power of the Holy Spirit on lay renewal weekends, deeper life conferences, and other renewal events. Indeed, the good news of Jesus Christ is coming alive in a grass roots spiritual awakening.

This spiritual awakening which is evangelizing the lost and dynamically renewing the Christian is quietly moving from person to person, church to church, and denomination to denomination. When an apathetic Christian finds new life and joy in his Christian life those around him notice his changed life and are drawn closer to Christ. One man in Orlando, Florida, committed his life to Christ after observing the renewed fellowship of the First Baptist Church, Pinecastle, Florida. Driving by the church on Sunday morning of their renewal weekend, the man observed the church members on the front lawn relating to one another in evident Christian love. He said to himself, "I would like to be a part of that fellowship." The next day he drove to the church, walked up to the entrance of the sanctuary and posed the following question to the custodian, "Is God in there?" The custodian directed him to the pastor who led him to Jesus Christ.

As people are being renewed they are finding that they are on an exciting new journey into the discovery of (1) a deeper and more meaningful spiritual life, (2) a more meaningful relationship within the church and the Christian community, and (3) a more fruitful sharing of the good news of Jesus Christ as they go into their own worlds—schools, neighborhoods, and businesses.

This new journey is a part of the basic journey which every Christian begins when he commits his life personally to Jesus Christ. However, it is new in the sense that many Christians have been stalled at some particular point along the way. They now have begun to move to new levels and areas of the Christian life. For example, many fine Christians are stalled at the spectator state of the Christian life. Through renewal God is setting them on their feet again. He is moving them toward participation in the ministry of the church rather than filling a pew and praying for the pastor to do the ministry for them.

As people begin to move from stalled positions they are discovering that God is doing more than giving them a "shot in the arm." Churches are discovering that it is a new journey in which people and churches begin where they are and move to new levels. It is an exciting journey with Jesus and his friends—the people of God!

Wake Up and Live!

> Why all this stress on behavior? Because, as I think you have realized, the present time is of the highest importance—it is time to wake up to reality. Every day brings God's salvation nearer.
>
> The night is nearly over; the day has almost dawned. Let us therefore fling away the things that men do in the dark, let us arm ourselves for the light of the day! Let us live cleanly, as in the daylight, not in the "delights" of getting drunk or playing with sex, nor yet in quarreling or jealousies. Let us be Christ's men from head to foot, and give no chances to the flesh to have its fling (Rom. 13:11-14, Phillips).

Today the people of God are poised around the world in strategic positions to touch a lost, hurting, and broken world with the love and healing balm of our Lord. The Holy Spirit is moving through spiritual renewal, awakening the people of God with the call to wake up and live!

Bill Cheshire of the First Baptist Church of Pompano Beach, Florida, is one of the people of God who responded to God's call to wake up and live on a lay renewal weekend at the First Baptist Church of Deerfield Beach, Florida.

Bill was flying around in circles of conformity to the expectations of both the secular and Christian communities. In the Christian community he was attending and giving. In the secular community he maintained a successful image as a professional and met the demands of local society by "living the life of Riley." In the Christian community he was a faithful church member, yet he was only nominally committed to the lordship of Jesus Christ. In the secular community he was enjoying external success while overextending himself by launching out into the cattle business. The cattle business began to have troubles, and Bill's secular world began to crumble.

Bill went through a living hell as he was squeezed in the vise of financial pressure. He who had always been independent and capable of paying his own way was forced to seek financial aid from those close to him. When he had been turned down on every hand, Bill became desperately depressed. At a moment of great crisis Bill turned to God as a last resort. The heavy burden of depression was lifted and from that point on Bill was slowly led out of the wilderness of financial ruin. It was following this experience that Bill was invited to participate as a member of the visiting team for the lay renewal weekend at Deerfield Beach.

On Friday night the coordinator for the weekend called upon Bill to give his testimony, not really knowing what he had been through. Bill very honestly related the story of his spiritual life. He recalled that success had been a way of life for him—at military school, in the Marines, and later in Pompano in his chiropractic practice. He had felt a great deal of pride in his success, enjoying his image as a self-made man, and not feeling any need for a deeper relationship with God. Yet his recent financial desperation had driven him to turn to God, who had not turned him down. As Bill related the incidents of his first major failure, his subsequent spiritual victory, and the great things God had done for him, he was suddenly overcome with the realization of God's love for him just as he was. This tough, self-made man broke down and wept. That night Dr. Bill Cheshire quit flying in circles of conformity and landed to commit his life to the lordship of Jesus Christ.

Was Bill's commitment lasting? Did he continue the journey with Jesus? Did he ever! Bill found that he hungered to serve God. He accepted the nomination to become a deacon of his church, which he had refused a few short months before. He took Jesus into his practice and continually reported that patients were accepting Jesus Christ as their Savior and also finding healing and wholeness by the ministry of the Lord through him. Nine years later Bill is still ministering to his patients both physically and spiritually in the name of Jesus.

I shall never forget my friend, Tom Crider, asking me one morning what we had experienced the night before as we had sat in a circle of fellowship in Bill's house. I replied, "We experienced *koinonia*, which is real Christian fellowship." As I look back, I can see Dr. Cheshire, flying in circles around real commitment until one night through verbalizing his own testimony in a Christian community of love and acceptance he landed and raised a banner over his total life that proclaimed, "Jesus is Lord."

Spiritual Landing Strips for Searching Laymen

All Scripture is inspired by God . . . that the man of God may be adequate, equipped for every good work" (2 Tim. 3:17, NASB).

Bill Cheshire is a challenge to the church. Spiritually awakened and hungry to journey on with Jesus into ministry and witness, Bill greatly needed equipping. In these exciting days of the renewal of the laity, there are some important spiritual landing strips emerging for awakened laymen who are searching for more depth and reality in their Christian experience. Events such as lay renewal weekends, renewal retreats, and deeper life conferences have provided opportunities for personal growth in a variety of areas such as prayer, Bible study, interpersonal relationships, and ministry.

One such spiritual growth group in Louisiana had been meeting for two years when I visited one night. As the group met, the following things took place: A request was made for two bus drivers for the church's bus ministry from within the group. The group was asked to claim "another offshore oil rig." One of the group members, strengthened by the growth and fellowship of the group, had joined a friend in involving every member of an offshore oil rig in Bible study. Now the two were moving to another oil rig, hence this request to claim another oil rig for Bible study.

One couple emotionally and sincerely requested that the group uphold them as they sought the leadership of the Lord in accepting or rejecting a promotion with an oil firm.

The group rejoiced and wept together as one of its members, a divorcee with three children, related a personal experience of being ministered to by the group. She had no washing machine or dryer. One night the group showed up at her house with both washing machine and dryer, and the men of the group hooked them up with love and best wishes for a happy Christian life.

Varieties of renewal conference centers have emerged as spiritual landing strips for both searching laymen and pastors. For several years Findley Edge of the Southern Baptist Theological Seminary has been inviting searching Christians to renewal conferences at the Vineyard Conference Center in Louisville, Kentucky, directed by William Clemmons. Many have returned from such conferences to launch their churches on renewal journeys.

One of the most exciting spiritual landing strips being developed today is LAOS Institute—a drive-in equipping station for laymen and pastors. Several years ago Mickey Evans, then pastor of Dunklin Memorial Baptist Church of Indiantown, Florida, was led by God to go out into the wilderness between Okeechobee and Stuart, Florida, and build a "City of Refuge."

With faith and a machete, Mickey waded into this wilderness area and began to build a camp. His first clients were alcoholics, "no-bodies" of society. Mickey began to study how to help these "bottomed-out" men. He became exposed to the concepts of the ministry of the laity, relational theology, small group process, integrity therapy, the deeper life—in general the same areas that were opening in lay renewal. He began to tell the alcoholics that he was doing more than drying them out. He was preparing them for ministry in small groups to other alcoholics when they got back home.

While there were some disappointments and failures, many men did become ministers to their fellow alcoholics and in becoming ministers they became "somebodies."

As Mickey saw what was happening to the alcoholics, he began to see what God had been trying to teach him by having him build the "City of Refuge"—that the church is not for spectators to fill the church each Sunday to cheer on the pastor. The church is a repair shop to repair those who come to church so that they might leave as whole persons ready to penetrate their world for Jesus Christ.

Mickey began to invite people from the churches where he had ministered to come to the camp and become equipped on weekends to penetrate their worlds for Jesus Christ. Now LAOS Institute, a drive-in equipping station where hundreds of laymen and pastors from the churches in south and central Florida come each year to be equipped, is rising on the grounds of the camp which first began as a vision of a "City of Refuge."

Several churches are emerging as spiritual landing strips for laymen searching for equipping in the Christian life. One of the most prominent of these churches is the Church of the Saviour in Washington, D.C.

Another church which is a spiritual landing strip is the Heritage Baptist Church, Annapolis, Maryland. Under the leadership of its former pastor, David Haney, renewal was organized through large and small groups. Those committed to the renewal process were equipped by David in the large group and worked out their ministry and fellowship needs in the small groups.

Another landing strip which God is using is individual laymen. A couple of years ago God told Frank Jean, a Chinese missionary in Korea, to go to Boston. "Boston! Why, I don't even know where Boston is." Yet, on faith and hearing the word of God, Frank and his wife Ingrid made their way to Boston as missionaries to the United States. They discovered that God wanted them to build a spiritual landing strip in the United States for awakened and searching laymen.

The Jeans are now sharing their vision with students and corporation executives in the Massachusetts area. Their vision is that God is reopening China to Christian missionaries. However, this time the missionaries will be American corporation employees sent by their own companies, which are now negotiating to establish businesses in China. Much of the Jeans' ministry is equipping Christians for this missionary venture of discipling others in the Christian faith.

Recently one of Frank's New England friends, a Harvard lawyer named Bill, moved into a law firm in Atlanta, Georgia. While he is still a long way from China, Bill is implementing what Frank taught him as he disciples young adults and leads a prayer group in the office of this prominent law firm in Atlanta. The fellowship and ministry of the Jeans is an important landing strip, equipping searching laymen to live out God's will for their lives.

A Vision of the New Journey

> And it shall be in the last days, God says, that I will pour forth of my Spirit upon all mankind; and your sons and your daughters shall prophesy, and your young men shall see visions, and your old men will dream dreams (Acts 2:17, NASB).

There are beautiful visions being born out of the grassroots renewal movement. There is the vision that Jesus is Lord of every area of the Christian's life and over the total program of the church. On a recent lay renewal weekend at the First Baptist Church of Norcross, Georgia, a businessman named Dan, who had been investing in land around Atlanta, yielded to the lordship of Jesus Christ and declared publically he was giving his land to the Lord. In the few short months since then, Dan and a few interested businessmen have become deeply involved in developing a retreat center one hour from the heart of Atlanta to be used principally to provide a ministry to "drop-out" teenagers in the greater Atlanta area. When Dan got a vision of the lordship of Jesus Christ over his land investments, he saw possibilities beyond anything he had ever dreamed before. It is a pleasure to be with Dan as he shares his dream and celebrates the vision of his Lord.

There is the vision of the unlimited potential of laymen: "For you once were not a people, but now you are the people of God; you had not received mercy, but now you have received mercy" (1 Peter 2:10, NASB).

As renewal has spread across the United States, thousands of lay people are hearing their name called by God into meaningful ministries.

I heard my name! Seventeen years ago I was a layman circling true commitment to the Lord Jesus Christ. God led my wife and me to the First Baptist Church of Deerfield Beach, Florida. In my circling I was conforming to the expectations of society. I was building the image of a "good father and good husband." I was growing in community leadership through civic clubs and other involvement as well as enjoying increasing success in business circles. At the same time, I was quickly building a reputation as a faithful church member, yet I was really only circling the field.

Over a period of time a real hunger for spiritual reality developed in my life. I spent hours discussing spiritual things with my pastor, Robert Rowe. He is one of God's great equippers. He let me come to him in my doubts, ignorance, and confusion. He gently led me deeper into the Word of God, and I heard my name called to let Jesus be the Lord of my total life. On one occasion in prayer meeting the reality of the Holy Spirit came upon me, and suddenly I realized that the living God was present and wanted to control my life completely.

As I began to follow the Lord more fully, the hunger for a more meaningful Christian life grew. One afternoon I had one of the most dramatic experiences of my life. I was in my insurance office in the midst of my normal routine when suddenly I became keenly aware of the presence of the Holy Spirit. After a tremendous experience with God, I emerged with the conviction that God was calling me to leave my business and go to seminary to be equipped as a minister of Jesus Christ. I had heard my name called again! I went home to share with my wife, Phyllis, only to learn that for some time she, too, had been receiving the same leadings to leave our business and prepare for ministry. It was not necessarily a call to the pastorate or foreign missionary service. It was a call to an open agenda, a call to prepare for ministry and let God write the program. We were ultimately led to Southeastern Baptist Theological Seminary in Wake Forest, North Carolina. With our young son and infant daughter we spent one wonderful year there before family and business pressures called us back to Florida.

The year at Southeastern was a much needed year of equipping. God had given me a very valuable exposure to one of his fine equipping stations. I left with some valuable tools for Christian growth that were to be very important as I later became involved in lay renewal.

Within the next few years I would hear my name called time after time to come up on the mountaintop with God's chosen equippers including Findley Edge, (the patron saint of Southern Baptist renewal), Bruce Larson, (the patron saint of interdenominational renewal), and many others. As I look back, I marvel how God has led me, an ordinary layman involved in the insurance business, step by step to assume the leadership of the extraordinary ministry of Renewal Evangelism for the Home Mission Board of the Southern Baptist Convention. I have been charged with calling out and equipping thousands of hungry laymen. My hope and vision is that if God could call out my name—Mr. Very Ordinary, "Hang Loose" Hardin, and get me on mission—then anyone can follow Jesus into mission!

Conclusion

I shall never forget a statement during the lay renewal weekend evaluation service at the First Baptist Church of Baytown, Texas. More than once it was said, "If God can use that 'bunch' of ordinary folks from Florida in such a dynamic way, then surely he can use us, too." This is the vision of the full potential of the people of

God—millions who were once ordinary "nobodies" becoming minis-tering "somebodies," reconciling the world to God through Jesus Christ.

What a vision!—the church of Jesus Christ equipping God's new ministers, all of the people of God. People are answering his call to ministry with the only limitation being the availability and re-sponse of his people to the call to ministry and discipleship.

10

The Lord of My Life

George E. Worrell

EVANGELISM DIVISION, BAPTIST GENERAL CONVENTION OF TEXAS, DALLAS, TEXAS

One of the distinguishing marks of the renewal movement is its emphasis on the lordship of Christ. David Haney in his book, *Breakthrough into Renewal,* states that renewal is an idea and its object is the recovery of the New Testament concept of the laity. That is, *all* believers are *ministers,* and the *pastor's* ministry is to "equip the ministers." Renewal includes an emphasis on commitment to Christ as Lord, on finding one's own particular ministry, and on the necessity of witness.[1]

This one thing is true: Christ never for a moment dreamed of building an imperishable empire without securing from his followers an incomparable devotion. His challenge to his disciples was cast in terms of extreme sovereignty and control: "Forsaketh not all that he hath"; "Let him deny himself, take up his cross"; "whosoever hate not his father and mother"; "whosoever puts his hand to the plow and looks back is not fit for the Kingdom of God"; "whosoever saves his life will lose it. Whosoever will lose his life for my sake . . . will find it." Here are the Master's demands—finalities, ultimatums, commands—the last word in sovereignty.

What does "Lord" mean? Webster says, "Lord is one having power and authority over others." John Corts, with the Billy Graham Evangelistic Association, has suggested several shades of meaning in the word.

Relationship

Lordship means relationship. We are related to Him. Some words in the English language reflect relationship: husband, wife, son, daughter. Other words reflect occupation: policeman, student, manager. The word "Lord" is a word of relationship. In John 15:5 Jesus makes clear the absolute quality of that relationship. He said, "I am the vine, ye are the branches: He that abideth in me, and I in him, the same bringeth forth much fruit: for without me ye can do nothing."

With five children in my family, we have a food crisis. Every year we seek to grow a big garden. Last year we planted some rhubarb next to our bedroom window. I was delighted to see that the leaves were almost as big as elephant ears. But as the summer went by, some of the leaves began to turn yellow around the edges. They wilted and finally died. I was so upset about it I almost performed an autopsy on those plants. I knew what was wrong. It was the relationship between the leaf and the root.

Some Christians are like that. Their Christian lives are turning yellow around the edges. They are wilting. Their faith is like a Pepsi that has lost its fizzle. Their faith is like cold gravy poured over mashed potatoes. The problem is that of relationship. They have accepted Jesus Christ as Savior of their lives, but they have not made Christ the Lord of their daily lives.

Remember, it is not very difficult to live a Christian life . . . it is absolutely impossible. Only as Christ as Lord lives out his life in us can we have a truly Christian life-style.

Ownership

Lordship means ownership. We belong to Him. There are many today who like to live their lives based upon the philosophy found in Henley's poem "Invictus." "I am the captain of my own soul"—I am the boss of my own life. This sounds profound, but it breaks down in every area of life. For instance, it breaks down in school. Suppose a teacher assigns an essay to be written on a certain subject and to be turned in on a certain day. Suppose the student says, "I am the captain of my own soul. I will write an essay if I choose on whatever subject I please. I will turn it in if I get ready." That student would make an *F*.

This philosophy breaks down in sports. Suppose you are a wide receiver on a football team. The quarterback calls a play in which you are to go down the middle and cut to the right. You say, "I am the captain of my own soul. I will go down the middle and cut to the left." You would not be playing on the football team. You would be sitting on the bench. This idea, "I am the captain of my own soul" breaks down in the home and in Christianity. Paul said in 1 Corinthians 6:19-20: ". . .ye are not your own? For ye are bought with a price: therefore glorify God in your body, and in your spirit, which are God's."

When a person becomes a Christian, he forfeits the right to do what he pleases, to say what he pleases, to go where he wants, to think what he wants, and to marry whomsoever he chooses. He must go where God wants him to go. He must be what God wants him to be. He must do what God wants him to do. He must think what God wants him to think. He must marry whomsoever it pleases God for him to marry. Some person might say, "Isn't this rather harsh?" Perhaps so, but this is the meaning of lordship. Christ is to have final authority over all of our lives. He is to be our boss, our manager, our captain, our Lord.

Devotion

Lordship means devotion. In Exodus 20:3, the Bible says, "Thou shalt have no other gods before me." A youth might say, "I have no fat-bellied Buddha upon a shelf which I worship." True, but some bow down before rock music and worship it as their god. Parents may say: "Sock it to the youth, preacher. Sock it to them." Yet, many a man has made his business his god. Many women have worshiped their children. Listen, God does not want *a* place in your life, He wants *first* place in your life.

Making Him Lord

It is one thing to say that Christ should be Lord of life. It is another thing to tell how to make him Lord. There are several ways which will help.

First, confess Jesus as Lord. In Philippians 2:10-11, Paul says that the day is coming when by demand every knee shall bow and every tongue confess that Jesus Christ is King of kings and Lord of lords. However, Christ cannot be our daily Lord unless we make him so each day that we wait upon his final coming. Every day, every hour, every moment that self seeks to be on the throne of your heart, you must stop and confess, "Jesus, you are my Lord."

Secondly, make a spiritual inventory and place the things of your life under his control.

Place the precious things of your life under his control—your gems, your furs, your paintings, your valuable things. You must go further! When God determined the faithfulness of Abraham in Genesis 22, he asked for the most precious thing in his life—his young son Isaac. God will ask for the Isaacs in your life as well.

Place your personal things under his control. These are the things that seem to be ours and are withheld from all others. Give him your looks for instance. Some might say, "If I gave him my looks, he wouldn't have much." Remember, you, along with your looks are important to God. Place them and all other personal things under his control.

Place your problems under his control. Perhaps you have difficulty making a living. Place this under the control of God. Perhaps there is a generation gap within the family. Place that under the control of God. Perhaps you have a problem of relating to people. Place these people under his control. He can handle them better than you. He may even change you!

Place your possessions under his control. You say, "I have a house and car, but they really aren't mine. The bank and I own them." It is the Lord who gives you the time, energy, and breath to make the payments on your possessions. Place all of these under the control of the Lord.

Third, do not practice spiritual Indian giving. An Indian giver is one who gives something away. Then he changes his mind and takes it back. Watch for the symptoms of taking back. Observe the prominence of the personal pronoun—excessive use of the words "my" and "mine." Observe the priority of time and thought spent. Be careful of an improper amount of time spent on one specific subject of your list. Be aware of pressures that create tensions . . . areas of our lives where pressure indicates a clash of our wills with the will of God. Problem areas involving conflicts of emotion relationships, especially need to be yielded to his control.

Finally, hold nothing back. There is a beautiful pamphlet entitled, "My Heart—Christ's Home" written by Robert Boyd Munger. It describes a person who invites Christ into his heart. The young man gives Christ the key to his library which is his mind, to his living room which is his heart, to his dining room which is his stomach, to his workroom which is his hands. He reserves the right, however, to keep the key to a small room just a few square feet on the second floor.

One day the young man found Christ waiting for him at the door. There was an arresting look in his eyes as he said, "There is a peculiar odor in the house. There is something dead around here. It's upstairs and it's coming from the hall closet. Give me the key so that I can clean out the uncommitted things and sins that are stored there." The young man was angry. He had given Christ access to the library, dining room, drawing room, workshop, and now He was asking him about a little two-by-four closet. He said, "This is too much. I am not going to give you the key." "Well," said Christ, "if you think I am going to stay here on the second floor with this odor you are mistaken. I will take my bed out on the back porch." The Lord started down the stairs.

The young man followed Christ and said, "I'll give you the key, but you will have to open the closet and clean it out. I don't have the strength to do it."

"I know you don't," said Jesus. "Give me the key. Authorize me to take care of it and I will." With trembling fingers the young man passed the key to him. Christ took it from his hand. He opened the door and cleaned the closet in a moment's time. It was a victory and release for the young man.

That day the young man said to Christ, "Up to this point you have been the guest in my heart, I have been the host. From this day forward, I want you to be the host and I will be the guest."

On that same day, the young man took the title of the deed to his house and said: "Here is the deed to my home. All that I am and have forever. Now you run the house. I'll just remain with you as a houseboy and friend."

On that day Christ indeed became Lord.[2]

So it is! As we yield every item on our list to Christ, he controls it. As he controls our lives, the Spirit empowers us. He constantly makes it a greater joy to yield additional areas of our lives to him.

Conclusion

Louis Evans tells of a wanderer who came across a man preparing to drown a dog in a tow sack. "Say," said the wanderer, "why are you doing that?" "Mister," said the man, "this dog's name is Gypsy. He follows after everybody's wagon. Any dog that follows after everybody's wagon isn't any good to anybody in particular." "Mister," said the wanderer, "would you let me have that dog?" "I guess so, but he's no good." The wanderer tucked the little dog under his arm, threw his duffel bag over his shoulder and moved on. As he went he spoke to the dog, "Gypsy, you and I are two of a kind. I've been a Christian for a long time, but I've been following after everybody's wagon. I've given my allegiance first to this person and then to that person and sometimes to the Lord. You've helped me see how foolish all this is. From now on, we're going to change things. I'm going to be your master and Christ is going to be mine."

Let Christ be the Lord of your life!

Notes

[1] David Haney, *Breakthrough into Renewal* (Nashville: Broadman, 1974), p. 23.

[2] Adapted from *My Heart—Christ's Home* by Robert Boyd Munger. © 1954 by Inter-Varsity Christian Fellowship. Used by permission of Inter-Varsity Press.

II BIBLE STUDIES
George Worrell

Just why God chooses to move in certain directions at certain times cannot always be understood. Perhaps the people with whom he works become receptive to different emphases because of felt needs.

Not all of the texts in the Renewal Bible Study section contain the word renew. Yet the concepts are there ready and willing to bless both clergy and laity who are on the journey.

Dry Bones Can Live Again
Ezekiel 37:1-14

Ezekiel 37:1-14 records a vision given to the prophet Ezekiel. Ezekiel's name means "God strengthens." This prophet was a victim of the Babylonian captivity. He, along with his kinsmen, had lost their country, their capitol city, their service and independence as a nation. Their condition was lamentable and could be compared with a valley full of dry bones.

Ezekiel's vision was not the product of his own brain. It was the gift of God (v. 1). In his vision he saw a valley of human bones which were not arranged in human form (v. 2). They were scattered hither, thither, and yon—all kinds of them. They covered the valley floor like a strange grim growth. God questions the prophet, "Can these bones become people again?" Ezekiel responds, "You alone know the answer to that" (v. 3, TLB). Before his very eyes the dry bones are transformed into live human beings (vv. 4-10).

Verses 10-14 interpret the vision. Israel is the valley of dry bones which God is going to resurrect and return to its native land.

The hope that renewal is possible arises from the historical realism that new life has emerged in many different periods. The biblical basis of this hope goes back to the Hebrew Scriptures and is given its most vivid expression in the vision of the valley of dry bones. This vision epitomizes the combination of realism and hope, which must always be the stance of the people of God. What is really encouraging is that the vision has been enacted over and over in historical fact. Just when the darkness has seemed inpenetrable, new light has shined for generation after generation. Renewal is, therefore, based upon the universalized philosophy of resurrection.[1]

Renewal and Ethics
Psalm 51

In its superscription, Psalm 51 is identified with David when Nathan the prophet condemned the king for two horrendous sins. Upon conviction of his social crimes, David rushed to the tabernacle to plead for forgiveness. Psalm 51 represents his written confession. The theme of the chapter is "A Sinner's Prayer." Verses 1-9 contain David's prayer for forgiveness. In verses 10-12 David calls for restoration. Verses 13-17 set forth his holy resolutions.

One of the most important insights on renewal is found in verses 10-13. Here David prays, "Create in me a clean heart, O God; and renew a right spirit within me. Cast me not away from thy presence; and take not thy holy spirit from me. Restore unto me the joy of thy salvation; and uphold me with thy free spirit. Then will I teach transgressors thy ways; and sinners shall be converted unto thee."

Two key words in the chapter are found in verse 10. They are *create* and *renew*. David realized that his need was so deep it would require divine assistance. His old life forgiven but unchanged would produce only temporary results. If he was to have an effective remedy, it would have to come with a divine re-creation at the center of his being.

The word "renew" means "to make new." David did not desire

a restoration of what was there before. He wanted a radical change
of heart and spirit.

Important renewal insights are contained in the content progression
of Psalm 51. First, David confessed his sin and was forgiven. Second,
he was cleansed and renewed. Third, there was a compassion that
led to effective witnessing. David confessed his sin and said, "Then
will I teach transgressors your ways and sinners shall be converted
unto you."

There would be more compassion for the outsiders if more Christians were renewed to a cleansed vital relationship with God. Furthermore, the lost would listen better if, like David, Christians would
be vulnerable. We must admit to what the world already knows.
Christians are not perfect. They have problems. A lost person always
responds better to the message of Christ which comes from an
humble, open, and honest Christian.

The Spirit-filled Life
Ephesians 5:18

Renewal participants are aglow with the concept of the Spirit-filled
life. They hear about it and talk about it. Paul talked about it too
in Ephesians 5:18. He said, "And do not get drunk with wine, for
that is debauchery; but be filled with the Spirit."

There is a contrast in this verse between drunkenness and Spirit-filling. There is also a comparison. The comparison is in the matter
of control. A drunken person is controlled by the liquor which he
has consumed. The man who is Spirit filled is controlled by the
Spirit.

All Christians in their spiritual experience belong somewhere along
the scale between immaturity and maturity. First Corinthians 3:1-3
designates the immature Christian as carnal. Note that *The Living
Bible, Paraphrased* calls the carnal Christian a baby Christian. First
Corinthians 2:14-15 pictures the mature Christian as one who "has
the Spirit" (TEV). If a person is to progress toward maturity, he

must be controlled by the Holy Spirit. A person may be immature because he has been a Christian only for a short time. On the other hand, there are those who have been Christians for a long time but who are still immature, because they have not yielded control of their lives to the Holy Spirit.

Being filled with the Spirit is not extracurricular. It is a major course in life. The Greek word translated "be filled" in Ephesians 5:18 is in the imperative mood. It is a mandate which refers to an enduring, continuous action. Christians are expected to be filled with the Spirit.

The story is told of a small town that had an annual summer tent revival. Each summer one person in the little town would go to the altar and weep over his sins. He would pray, "Oh Lord, fill me with the Holy Spirit." Three months later he would be living in his old ways. At the next revival he would be down at the altar praying, "Oh Lord, fill me with the Holy Spirit, fill me with the Holy Spirit." At last, one elderly Christian said, " 'Tain't no use Lord, he leaks." His problem is our problem. We do not seek the infilling of the Holy Spirit often enough. Infilling cannot be a once-a-year, once-a-month, or once-a-week matter. It must be a once-a-day, once-an-hour, once-a-minute renewal.

Actually, our lives are not like glasses that have the Holy Spirit poured into us in various amounts at various times. Rather, the Holy Spirit on conversion makes his homestead in our heart. His control over our lives can be quenched or encouraged. Some Christians allow the Holy Spirit to possess them more fully than others. God's goal for all Christians is that all allow the Holy Spirit to control them completely.

The Pastor-equipper
Ephesians 4:11-12

In the King James version, Ephesians 4:11-12 reads, "And he gave some, apostles; and some, prophets; and some, evangelists; and some pastors and teachers; For the perfecting of the saints, for the work of the ministry, for the edifying of the body of Christ." This rendering of the Greek text is not the best. Instead of the preposition "for" being repeated three times the Greek says, *pros, eis, eis.* These prepositions would be better rendered: "for," "unto," "unto." A more literal translation would be that Christ has given pastors and teachers to the church "for the equipping of the saints *unto* the work of the ministry, *unto* the upbuilding of the body of Christ."

This passage represents a cardinal feature of renewal. It indicates that not only does the Holy Spirit give special abilities to laymen for service, he also gives men as gifts to the body for its perfection. God has given some men the special ability for and the responsibility of being pastors and teachers to help laymen develop their own ministry. It must be made clear that it is always bad to make religion professional. However, it must also be clear that it is not wrong to make the pastor a professional. To be an equipping minister will require skill, knowledge, and great sensitivity. In this sense the minister ought to be a professional. He ought to be one who has a special ability in performing the kind of ministry which helps other people to perform their ministries. One word of caution, preachers should perform their ministry to equip the laymen. Laymen should not be jealous of this prerogative and seek to usurp the pastor-teacher's and evangelist's prerogative. The distinction between clergy and laity is not so much one of position as one of function. Each member of the body has a particular ministry. Being a pastor is but one of them. He is the equipping minister.

The Church a Unified Whole
1 Corinthians 12:12-13; Ephesians 4:1-3

The term "one body" is referred to four times in 1 Corinthians 12:12-13. Note the same reference in Romans 12:5 and Ephesians 4:4. The church denotes the whole body of true believers in Christ. Such believers include all of those on earth, in heaven, and in all ages. The church is composed of the saints of the past, the present, and the future. As a unified whole, the church is responsible to present a *unified front to the world* and a *fellowship of love to Christ.* On one occasion a pastor took a church that was beaten and scarred by inner strife. As he visited in the homes of the outsiders, he found that the church had lost its respect in the community. It took thirteen years for the church to regain its rightful position in the community. In the meantime, scores of lost people died without Christ.

The heart of Christ must be continually broken because of the parts of his body fighting against each other. No wonder Paul said that church members should endeavor to keep the unity of the Spirit in the bond of peace (Eph. 4:3). The keys to church unity are set out in Ephesians 4:2: (1) Be humble. How far does humility go? A Christian could get trampled. So get trampled. God can restore you. (2) Be gentle and patient. (3) Make allowances for each other's faults. Sometime ago a young ministerial student asked his pastor, "How can I be a good pastor to the people?" His answer was classic. "Allow for a major fault and a lot of minor faults in the lives of every person to whom you minister and keep sweet." (4) Be loving (1 Cor. 13, John 13:34-35). "Christians must be like Jesus and say, 'I don't care about me, all I care about is you.' " A popular renewal song goes, "It's love, it's love that makes the world go round." It is also love that is the key to church unity.

Community in Christ
Acts 2:42,44,45

One of the characteristic things about modern man is the loneliness. He is a solitary figure. Relationships have been cut off. The typical mid-twentieth-century person is uprooted and detached. Life has become a wasteland. Man finds himself alone. He is a lost person, estranged from his fellows.

The secular world which coveted emancipation now realizes that there must be a community of people if there is to be fulfillment and happiness. Christians realize that when it is said that our society is sick with loneliness and the representative man of the mid-twentieth century is lost, it really means that man is lonely and lost because man is separated from God. Men will find one another in true companionship and fellowship only when they find one another in God their maker and redeemer.

Acts 2:42 points out four principles that have become keys to renewal. These principles are study, fellowship, communion, and prayer. "And they continued steadfastly in the apostles' doctrine and fellowship, and in breaking of bread, and in prayers."

First, there was study. Christians found their unity and comradeship, their joy and peace in one another because they embraced the same truth. It was the truth about life and death, about the beginning and the end, about man and the universe, about sin and salvation, about heaven and hell. This Christ-delivered truth was their rallying point. They preached, and they listened. They taught, and they studied. They asked questions and answered them. Together they sought to know and to make known the doctrine of Christ. In this they were united.

The second thing which offered community was fellowship. The word describing the fellowship is *koinonia*. Koinonia has become almost a sacred word to contemporary Christians. This is easily understood since the church developed in terms of mutual sharing one Christian with another. Out of this came a sense of partnership and belonging. It was a fellowship of mutual self giving (Acts 4:32) and friendship.

The third thing stimulating the community was the breaking of bread. The expression most likely refers to the celebration of the Lord's Supper. Note verse 46 where the disciples broke bread from "house to house" in addition to worshiping in the Temple. This they did mindful of the request of their Lord so recently spoken, "This do in remembrance of me."

A final way in which the group of early Christians achieved community in Christ was through prayer. Prayer was the natural result of communion with Christ through the word and the Lord's

Supper. Prayer is the constant exercise of fellowship with God coming to more definite expression at certain times. Prayer is the whole atmosphere and climate of community in Christ. As one hymn puts it, "Prayer is the Christian's vital breath, the Christian's native air." Prayer is never really solitary. It embraces all those who are in Christ. Did not Jesus teach us to pray, "Our Father, who art in heaven"? A great writer once said, "Society is a partnership of the dead, the living, and the unborn." Yes, but that partnership is realized only by those who are in Christ, who in their prayers thrill to know that they are one with the redeemed of all ages and of all peoples, both on earth and in heaven and yet unborn. A Christian at prayer is never alone—he is a member of the vast family of God.

In other words, the real solution to the modern social problem— man's quest for community—is found in the church, the body of Christ.

A Fellowship of Concern
Acts 4:34-35

The spiritual community of the early Christians expressed itself in a certain physical and material way. Under the full power of their newfound experience in Christ, the early Christians shared their material possessions. The standard for living became not what a man rightfully had, but what he needed. Their love for one another was so great that they voluntarily made a drastic redistribution of their personal property. Interestingly enough, redistribution of property was not an entirely new thought for Jewish Christians. Such a principle had been established by God in the historic practice of the Jubilee Year. Once every fifty years, property was supposed to revert to its original owner. (See Lev. 25:10-13,28.) Community in Christ demonstrated that the law indeed had been fulfilled in him.

The material community of the early Christians says something to the present situation. One of the trends of human society through-out the world is toward the redistribution of wealth and economic sharing. This drive often is administered through government, in orderly fashion on some occasions and with revolutionary methods on others. The most radical form of redistributing wealth is communism. The argument sometimes has been advanced that the example of the early church favored the communistic effort. This is a great misunderstanding. A vast difference exists between the two. The early Christians shared voluntarily with one another. Communism uses force and violence. The early Christians maintained private property. Even when the possessions were sold, the money remained in the hands of the seller. The early Christians were obedient to the rule of Christ. Communism obeys what it calls dialectical materialism. All this may be summed up by pointing out that communism is utterly materialistic. It claims that a person can have the true community he craves only by material reconstruction. The church insists that the opposite is the case. Man can find true community only by spiritual reconstruction in Christ. This reconstruction then will have its material effects. This is renewal.

Being Transformed and Renewed
Romans 12:1-2

Chapter 11 finished the doctrinal portion of the book of Romans. Now Paul turns to a practical application of the truths which he has declared. In the remainder of the epistle, Paul declares that the Christian's life should be in keeping with the inward nature. The theme of Romans 12 is the Christian and sanctification. In dealing with this theme Paul sets forth the failure, the plea, and the result.

First note the failure. That the Roman Christians had failed to comprehend the doctrine of separation from the world is evident in Paul's words, "And be not conformed to this world" (v. 2). This verse indicates that some of the early Christians were being conformed to the standards of their day rather than living a life in keeping with their redeemed natures. Perhaps one of the greatest single tragedies of modern Christendom is that Christians have received Christ as Savior but they have lost their usefulness by allowing Satan to dwarf their spiritual lives. They are born again but have never grown in grace, knowledge, and service for Christ. They are trying to hold on to the secular world with one hand and the spiritual world with the other. As Christians they are miserable. No wonder Paul warned, "Don't let the world around you squeeze you into its own mold" (Phillips).

Second consider the plea. "I beseech you therefore, brethren, by the mercies of God, that ye present your bodies a living sacrifice, holy, acceptable unto God, which is your reasonable service . . . be ye transformed by the renewing of your mind" (vv. 1-2). Paul indicates that sanctification and renewal are a process. Having dedicated the body to God's service, Christians are to grow more and more in the likeness of God's holy nature.

This is seen in Paul's words, "be ye transformed." The word "transform" means to change the outward appearance so that it will correspond to the inward nature. Transform is the word used to describe Jesus' transfiguration. To the disciples Jesus had had the outward appearance of a human being. Suddenly his deity shone forth from within, transforming his own outward appearance to conform with his inner or true nature. So Christians are to allow their inner redeemed nature to shine forth through their outward appearance. This transformation will not be realized in a second of time. It will be accomplished through a process of yielding to the Holy Spirit. This is seen in Paul's phrase "by the renewing of your mind." The word *mind* includes not only mental processes but attitudes, imaginations, feelings, desires—all that is involved in the word *soul*. The Christian must present his body instantaneously but growth of the soul into the likeness of God will be a continuing process. As previously noted, the word renew means "the making new again." It is used only twice in the New Testament along with two uses of its verb form. In each instance, the renew refers to the operation of the Holy Spirit upon one already born again. As the Christian submits himself to the Holy Spirit who dwells in him, the Holy Spirit will day by day renew the Christian. He will enable the Christian to achieve victory over sin and yield the body more and more to God's service.

Note again that the words "be conformed and be transformed" are both in the passive tense. Someone is doing something to you. Either Satan is conforming the Christian to the age in which he lives or else the Holy Spirit is transforming the Christian into one whose redeemed inner nature shines forth through the outer expression of the body.

Lastly, note the result. Paul continues, "that ye may prove what is that good and acceptable and perfect will of God." The word "proved" is an infinitive of purpose. Carried to its final conclusion, it amounts to result. Few Christians are entirely ignorant of the Bible teaching as to the will of God. Our trouble is that we have not tried to consistently do his will.

As an exercise read the entire twelfth chapter of Romans. You say the things Paul tells you to do are too hard. In your present state of dedication that may be so but try one of them. You say you cannot return good for evil. Try it. You say that in honor you cannot prefer another. Try it. You say that you cannot bless those who persecute you. Try it. You say you cannot be transformed by the renewing of the mind. Try it. It may be hard at first but with each successful attempt the next will be easier. That's renewal.

Divine Order
1 Corinthians 12:14-20

The divine order for life is unity and diversity. This may be seen in the combination of differences in the human body. The body is one, but it has many parts. Paul used the human body to attack a problem in the church at Corinth that had to do with gifts of the Spirit. Difficulties had arisen over several things. Some deluded men claimed to be the special organs of the Spirit. Some were dissatisfied with the gifts they had received. They envied those whom they regarded as more highly favored. Others were inflated and made an ostentatious display of their extraordinary powers. Confusion arose because the various persons wanted to exercise their gifts at the same time.

In 1 Corinthians 12-14, Paul discussed the correction of these problems. In the process of dealing with the problem of gifts, Paul drew a striking analogy between the church and the human body. He stated several truths: first, the body is one organic whole because it is animated by one's spirit. The church is one because of the indwelling of the Holy Spirit as the principle of its life.

Second, the very idea of the body as an organization supposes diversity in unity. The same is true regarding the church. Members with distinctive personalities possess unique abilities and gifts.

Third, the members of the human body are mutually dependent. No one part exists for itself but for the body as a whole. Note the humor in the absurd agreements of the foot and the ear (vv. 15-17). The church has the same dependence of its members on one another.

Fourth, all members are interrelated. Illness or health in one member affects all the rest. The same is true of all persons of the church.

In summary, God has given each church member special capacities and functions. Each is needful to the other. Each should esteem and respect the other. Each should be solicitous of the other. Each should be concerned for the welfare of the whole.

Our Thing
1 Corinthians 12:21

First Corinthians 12:21 is amazingly contemporary. An emphasis on personal experience has been taken to mean that each man is a law to himself. People seem to suppose that everyone can "do his own thing," and that no rules for the game have been written. This is a serious misunderstanding. Individual experience is vital, but the common affirmation of the body of Christ must be the rule of faith.

Man Remolded
Jeremiah 18:4

Jeremiah is one of the most interesting and human of all the prophets. Born at Anathoth, a small village six miles north of Jerusalem, he prophesied during the reign of four Hebrew kings from 626 B.C. to the fall of Jerusalem in 586 B.C. His entry into public life coincides with King Josiah's discovery of a book of the law (Deuteronomy) which precipitated a religious renewal and reformation among the Israelites.

His book is replete with illustrations. The most impressive one is his experience at the place of a potter. He sees in the potter's house the whole story of renewal. Just as the potter remolds a marred vase, so God will remold Christians. Four biblical truths emerge. First, the divine potter has power over the human clay. Jeremiah was proclaiming the greatest and most neglected truth of all times— the sovereignty of God.

A second truth Jeremiah announced at the potter's house is that God has a plan for each of us.

Third, some vessels are marred. "Why is it," some say, "that if God is infinite in power that there are so many people who thwart his purposes? If God is good why is there so much suffering? Why are there so many people whose lives have been wrecked by sin?"

Why does the potter fail with some of the vessels he seeks to mold? It is not because he is not a master craftsman. It is not because he is negligent in his work. It is because there is something in the clay which will not yield itself to the master's touch. It is not pliable. It will not cooperate with the potter.

Finally, marred vessels can be remolded for the master potter's use. What did the potter do with the marred clay—throw it away? No, he reworked it. He took out the extraneous material, moistened it, and remade it for usefulness. This is divine renewal, and this is what God is doing in the hearts of lay people today.

Almost without exception those whose renewal testimonies are included in this book testify of being born in a Christian home and express deep appreciation for Christian parents. They tell of joining the church and being baptized at an early age. They usually were active in the church until they went away to college. Then many tell of straying from the church. The men tell of entering military service still only casually related to God. After military service they tell how they came back home, married, and then started back to church. Soon they were teaching a Sunday School class. Later they would serve on the finance committee and then be elected deacon.

Often they would say in their testimony, "I really didn't know what the Christian faith was all about, but because I knew what it meant to be successful I worked to make it go." Then in some way they had a deep personal encounter with Jesus Christ which transformed their lives. They experienced a turn-around.[2] They still attend church but now church is meaningful. Their service to Christ is effective. Their prayer habits and Bible study have been changed. To what or to whom may this change be attributed—to God who has remolded lives for the Master Potter's use.

Notes

[1] David Haney, *Renew My Church*, (Grand Rapids: Zondervan, 1972), p. 11.

[2] Findley B. Edge, "Renewal—What is It?" from *Lay Renewal Preparation Manual*, compiled by David Haney and Reid Hardin, (Atlanta: Home Mission Board), p. 6.

III ILLUSTRATIONS

AFFIRMATION

. . . Man lives by affirmation even more than by bread.—(**12**,63)

. . . Ever feel like a frog? Frogs feel slow, low, ugly, puffy, drooped, pooped. I know. One told me. The frog feeling comes when you want to be bright but feel dumb, when you want to share but are selfish, when you want to be thankful but feel resentment, when you want to be great but are small, when you want to care but are indifferent.

Yes, at one time or another each of us has found himself on a lily pad floating down the great river of life. Frightened and disgusted, we are too froggish to budge. Once upon a time there was a frog. But he really wasn't a frog. He was a prince who looked and felt like a frog. A wicked witch had cast a spell on him. Only the kiss of a beautiful maiden could save him. But since when do cute chicks kiss frogs? So there he sat, unkissed prince in frog form. But miracles happen. One day a beautiful maiden grabbed him up and gave him a big smack. Crash! Boom! Zap!! There he was, a handsome prince. And you know the rest. They lived happily ever after. So what is the task of the Church? To kiss frogs, of course.—(**12**,11-12)

. . . God didn't ask us to see through each other but to see each other through.

. . . Ever since I saw the musical play, *Man of La Mancha*, my patron saint has been Don Quixote. It is the story of a senile old man who sets off to do battle with evil in the world. Hundreds of years after the death of chivalry, he dons a rusty suit of armor and goes forth to right wrongs.

His companion is a fat, funny, little fellow named Sancho Panza. To Don Quixote, Sancho is the squire of a great knight. Knowing that he

NOTE: Throughout this section the figures at the end of most quotations refer to the sources (boldface type) in the list on page 140 and to the page numbers (lightface type) in those sources.

is only a humble servant on the old man's farm, Sancho nevertheless loves his master and enters into his fantasy. And so the two set off on their quest: Quixote on a horse and Sancho on a mule.

The two ride up to a broken-down inn where mule traders stop. When Don Quixote meets the slovenly innkeeper of this very questionable establishment—which is no Howard Johnson's Motor Lodge—he kneels before him and says something like: "Behold, you are the lord of this great manor. I ask you to knight me in the proper fashion." The innkeeper protests this obvious madness but Don insists.

At dinner with the mule traders, Don Quixote sees the poor, misused kitchen wench who comes in to serve the meal. In his eyes she is a pure and beautiful maiden. He asks her to give him a token of her purity that he may take into battle as he fights the forces of evil.

She insists vehemently that she is not a lovely maiden. In a deeply moving song she tells of having been born in a ditch and of having been used and abused by hundreds of men. Again the Don refuses to see the reality of the situation and declares that he must have a token from the pure girl.

The story continues in this vein, contrasting Quixote's holy madness with the brutal facts of the real world. At the end, the old man is once again back in his bed at home, dying. Now he is in his right mind and no longer believes that he is a knight. The most moving scene of the play is enacted when the people he has encountered come to his bedside and beg him not to change. For in a strange and miraculous way, each one has become a new person: the person whom Quixote saw in his pure and noble fantasy.

This is the power that you and I have if we love in the way that Jesus Christ has loved us. Our Lord calls us to a kind of "La Mancha madness." He wants us to go into the world and call people forth, to call them by their true names which may be deeply hidden. He calls us to affirm people.—(14,53-55)

. . . *How do you see yourself?* Is your name Timid, or Dishonest, or Self-conscious, or Fearful, or Indifferent, or Reserved? The name by which God calls you might be just the opposite. It may be that your real name is Courageous, or Faithful, or Warm, or Generous.—(13,21)

. . . Lazarus, wrapped in graveclothes, hands and arms bound to his sides, hobbles out of the tomb at the command of our Lord. Jesus, by the power of God, gives life to the dead man. But the intriguing thing comes next. He turns to the friends nearby and says to them, "Loose him and let him go." You see, it is Jesus who gives life to the dead, but it is fellow Christians who are instructed to loose and unbind those who have begun to find life. We release those who have found life in Christ by our concern or we bind them by our indifference. Taking off the bandages can become the most exciting ministry of all.—(12,18)

. . . The world has beat my people down all week; they don't need me to add to it, they need to be *lifted!*—(8,6)

. . . One of my favorite Scripture passages is Job 4:4 in Moffatt's translation. It is one of Job's friends saying to Job: "Your words have kept men on their feet." Perhaps as much as anything, that is our mission within the circle of Christian fellowship. "Let us encourage one another."—(9,30)

. . . There are two kinds of people on earth today,
Just two kinds of people, no more, I say,
Not the good and the bad, for 'tis well understood
The good are half bad and the bad are half good.

Not the happy and sad, for the swift flying years
Bring each man his laughter and each man his tears.
Not the rich and the poor, for to count a man's wealth
You must first know the state of his conscience and health.

Not the humble and proud, for in life's busy span
Who puts on vain airs is not counted a man.
No! The two kinds of people on earth I mean
Are the people who lift, and the people who lean.—(21)

. . . The gift of a listening ear and an understanding heart is sometimes the greatest gift one Christian can give another.

. . . Unhappy, depressed, a young woman on her way to a teaching job in East Chicago, Indiana, read a newspaper announcement of the annual scholarship competitions at Chicago School of Music. Yielding to a forlorn hope, she arranged for an audition.

Waiting her turn in the contest, she was dismayed by the highly professional vocalizing of her competitors. When finally her summons came from Edourado Sacerdote, celebrated operatic coach, she approached the piano with fear and trepidation.

As she launched into her song, the youthful singer's voice quavered. She cast an anguished glance at Sacerdote. He looked at her and winked! It said to her plainly: You're doing great. Don't be afraid. Everything will come out all right.

Instantly her hopes soared, her fears were forgotten. And she won the scholarship!

Thus did a friendly wink change the life of a frightened young woman. Irene Dunne had started up the ladder of fame.—Adrian Anderson

BEARING BURDENS

. . . The New Testament lays heavy emphasis upon the need for Christians to know each other, closely and intimately enough to be able to bear one another's burdens, confess faults one to another, rebuke, exhort, and admonish one another, minister to one another with the word and through song and prayer.

BIBLE READING

. . . Bible reading will be much more more effective if a person will write the following questions in the flyleaf of the Bible. Then be guided by them as the Bible is read: Is there a sin to avoid? truth to learn? prayer to echo? duty to perform? sin to confess? promise to claim?—(9,38)

. . . A very talented young minister friend of mine was quite eager to stimulate his congregation's interest in the reading of the Bible. He announced that on a certain Sunday night there would be a vote taken to determine what portions of the Bible would be left in and what portions would be taken out. The poll was made, not on the basis of what they believed, but on the basis of what they had read. Those passages which the majority of the people had read during the previous year would remain, but those passages which the majority had not read would be removed. They began with Genesis and moved all the way through the Bible. It was a rather traumatic experience for the congregation. Genesis 1, the Ten Commandments in Exodus, one or two favorite passages from Isaiah, the Twenty-Third Psalm, portions of the Sermon on the Mount, the third and fourteenth chapters of John, and First Corinthians 13 were the passages which survived.

The congregation got the point. It is not the Bible believed, but the Bible believed and read which has the potential for changing lives. One individual rushed up to the minister after the service and said, "I deplore your tearing pages out of God's Holy Word in front of the church." Evidently the mutilating of the pages bothered her more than the neglect of the reading and the teaching of the Scripture.—(4,46-47)

. . . If you doubt that the Bible is relevant I challenge you to do this:

buy a very inexpensive copy of the New Testament in an up-to-date translation. Remove the back and cover, and divide it into thirty equal parts. Put each section together with a paper clip or a staple. You can put them where they will be noticed each morning, then during the day as you are waiting on someone, instead of working yourself into a lather, just pull out your little packet and read until he comes. The average husband could read through the Bible every year during the time he spends waiting for his wife. The average wife could read through the New Testament using the time that she waits for her husband to get to the dinner table. Learning what the Bible means and how to apply it to life is our main goal, but first we must learn what it says. I challenge you simply to expose yourself to the Word of God.—(4,49)

CARNAL CHRISTIANS

. . . In a suburb of a large town, a pastor lived across the street from a fifty-year-old man who had the mind of a two-year-old. His parents had to discipline him, take care of his needs, and treat him as a child. This is abnormal.

It is also abnormal for a person to be born into the kingdom of God and never grow in Christ. The carnal Christian is the Christian who has never grown. He is the Christian who has never allowed the Holy Spirit to have control over his life.

. . . Carnal Christians are like the little girl who fell out of bed, explaining, "I guess I fell asleep too close to where I crawled in."—(19,147)

. . . The carnal Christian tries to hold on to the secular world with one hand and to the spiritual world with the other. Consequently, he develops a split personality. This, in turn, brings tremendous unhappiness. Have you ever seen a person who professes to be a Christian and, yet, is unhappy? This person is most likely a carnal Christian, experiencing a civil war in his heart. It is as Galatians 5:17 says, "For the flesh lusteth against the spirit, and the spirit against the flesh: And these are contrary the one to the other; so that ye cannot do the things that ye would."

CHRISTIAN MORAL LIFE

. . . Many times people say that "living the life" is being a witness. Others say that "speaking verbally about Jesus" is being a witness. In the case of evangelism it is not a matter of either one. It is a matter of both. Living a moral life and sharing the spoken word go together. You cannot separate them. If you have one without the other, your witness is incomplete.

Just as an airplane has two wings, so your witness has two parts: the life you live and the words you speak. If you are flying at thirty thousand feet and the pilot says one of our wings has to be dropped, which one do you want to drop—the left one or the right? It would be a disaster to drop either one of them. As long as you are flying, neither should be dropped. This is true with our witness. Both living and talking about the Lord are mandatory. One cannot drop either without "crashing."

. . . Recently I entered into a partnership arrangement with a lifetime friend of mine. We were together almost every Saturday for the past few months. He had the habit of talking vulgarly and using the Lord's name in vain extensively. He confided that he had noticed that I never used any bad language in my conversation and seemed to be able to talk just as well as he. With this opening, I shared that I had noticed his language but had hesitated to say anything about it. I told him that I felt that kind of language was in poor taste and usually indicated a lack of vocabulary for those who used it. About three weeks later he again confided that he had discussed this problem with his wife and was going to make a determined effort to refrain from using this type of language in the future. In fact, he encouraged me to correct him if he slipped and said something while we were together.

This incident is but another illustration that how we live and talk is important. We sometimes witness in more ways, either good or bad, than we are aware of at the time. Quite often being able to witness at the right moment, when completely unexpected, is the very best way.—Bill F. Davis, First Baptist Church, Wylie, Texas.

. . . Christianity does not consist in abstaining from doing things no gentleman would think of doing, but consists of doing things that are unlikely to occur to anyone who is not in touch with the spirit of Christ.—(3,66)

. . . The only exposure of converts to the Christian community will occur through you and your friends. The revelation of just how transformed a Christian life can be will be revealed primarily through you. As you are being changed into his likeness, from "one degree of glory to another" (2 Cor. 3:18, RSV), the "pilgrim" in you will encourage your friend to proceed on his pilgrimage. Hunger for God can be created in others only when you carry the imprint of God clearly without your own person. Your new concert from the world of Outsiders will watch, and watch, and watch . . . you! Do you bear watching?

. . . There is one tremendous answer to this problem: *we must help one another!* No individual can see very far in the encircling darkness, but as Robert Barclay recognized three hundred years ago, several small candles may make a great light. "As many candles lighted and put in one place," he wrote, "do greatly augment the light, and make it more to shine forth, so when many are gathered together in the same life, there is more of the glory of God and His power appears, to the refreshment of each individual." I believe that this is true, and that this is why there cannot be any vital Christianity without an increased sense of being members one of another. I know that groups may fail, but I also know that there is no power without them. Neither I nor anyone else can be a Christian alone.—(11,7)

CHURCH

. . . A person reared away from other persons never develops. A Christian who attempts to grow without the help of other Christians will be a disappointment. One cannot grow and develop in isolation. People need people. We help one another to grow.—(4,38)

. . . However bad the Church may be, the alternative of a churchless world is manifestly worse.—(10,13)

. . . The church is here on earth, not to do what other groups can do, but to do what no other group of human beings can possibly do.—(22)

. . . Christ never intended the church to be like a beehive with a queen bee, workers, and drones! He intended it to be like a body with functioning parts and every part functioning!—(7,70)

. . . To minister in our society, we need not so much the ministry of the ordained as we do the ministry of the laity. It is the laymen exercising their faith in this technical and complex, bureaucratic and impersonal society who will truly proclaim the gospel.—(6,112)

. . . A famous Methodist once said, "Various people have been placing the church in a casket for centuries. The only hang-up is, they've never been able to bury it.

. . . The church, in its high times and its lows, always and ever exists to function, not merely to exist.—(8,36)

. . . The average church fellowship is so respectable that real problems never come out into the open.—(11,13)

. . . The church should be in the world. It is only thus that the world will understand that Christ is not dead, is not gone, and is not inactive.— (22,94)

CHURCH PROGRAM

. . . Carl Bates says that the Holy Spirit could withdraw from the church and ninety-five percent of our work would go on—and we would brag about its success!—(10,80)

CHURCH WORK

. . . It is an unwritten law of religious work that the more responsibility a pastor assumes, the more a congregation will let him assume.—(16,87)

COMMUNION WITH GOD

. . . When Paul exhorted the Thessalonian believers to "pray without ceasing," he was not referring simply to the frequency of the act of saying prayers, not just to persevering in prayer. He was, instead, speaking of prayer as an attitude and state of heart, involving one's very life and daily walk. A life of fellowship with God! Life is spontaneous, like the beating of the heart. My heart does not beat because I choose and will that it should beat, but it beats spontaneously, by the volition and operation of God. Prayer is to be just like that. Prayer is the breathing of the spirit. I do not breathe by volition or deliberate choice. I just breathe naturally and automatically; it is in the very nature of my life to breathe. Christians should live at this state in the experience of prayer. Communion and fellowship with God ought to be to the spiritual life what breathing is to the physical life.—(5,21)

CONFESSION

. . . Sin does not break our relationship with God, but it does damage it. Sin alienates and separates us from God. When we sin, it is as if we have put a brick on a wall between us and God. The effect is the same as if somebody unplugged the power cord. We lose our power source.

The only solution to sin in the Christian life is confession. Confession restores us to a right relationship with our Father. It brings us into complete harmony and fellowship with Him.

A couple constantly fought and fussed. Finally the pastor said to the woman, "My soul, Margaret, why do you and your husband constantly fight?" The wife replied, "It is true, pastor. We do fight, but it sure is fun to make up."

The way we make up with God is by confession of sin.

. . . We can be confessors one to another and thereby tap a dimension of God's Holy Spirit that can bring healing to all those who are willing to know and be known.—(**12**,51)

. . . A frustrated young clergyman, conscious of sin and failure in his own life, found the senior minister of his church busy, so he asked the building superintendent to hear his confession and pray with him for forgiveness. These two men knew each other only superficially, but they had a common love for Jesus Christ and the church. The sexton agreed to the request on condition that he also be given the chance to make his confession.

When the two men got off their knees they found themselves brothers, and they agreed to meet together again soon to renew the experience. They quickly thought of others in the parish who needed the cleansing and the benediction which God had given them, and then and there a Christian group was born.—(**11**,12)

. . . Most of us see the need to confess those acts that are blatantly wrong, but what about those things that are just a little dishonest and that can begin to erode our very integrity and personality?—(**12**,52)

CRITICISM

. . . There is an old saying that may come from one of our Indian tribes which goes like this: "Do not criticize your brother until you have walked a mile in his moccasins." Perhaps we would say it this way, "Do not criticize your brother until you have walked in his shoes." It is easy to criticize someone and say what we would do or would not do if we were in his or her position. But if we have not been in such a situation we do not know what we would do.—(**5**,53)

EQUIPPER

. . . Again, the basic idea is that the minister is not to be *the* preacher, *the* pastor, *the* prophet, *the* priest, and *the* administrator FOR his church. Instead, his task is to equip members of his congregation so that they might become preachers, pastors, prophets, priests, and administrators themselves.—(**16**,43)

. . . A layman said to me recently, "Your job is like that of a foreman in a plant. A foreman has a twofold responsibility, first he must teach and train his men to do their work; second, he is responsible for their production. He must watch over them guiding them and encouraging them to produce. So, you as a clergyman have to train us for our ministry, and then help us to fulfill our mission to produce. We are called to 'go and bear fruit'; you are called to see that we do it."—(20,142)

. . . The clergyman's abiding frustration is that in doing the many things that are useful, he may be prevented from doing the one thing needful. It is being suggested here that the one thing needful in the role of the clergyman for our time is that he prepare his people for their ministry in the church and in the world. The chief task of the clergyman is to equip his people for their ministry. All his work is to this end. The functions of preacher, prophet, pastor, priest, evangelist, counselor, and administrator find their proper places in the equipping ministry.

The purpose of this ministry is that the people shall be trained and outfitted for their work in the church and in the world.—(20,141)

. . . Even if a pastor *understands* that his primary role is to be that of equipping others for their ministry, he must then confront himself with the hard question: is this who I *want* to be? To be a "builder of community," "catalytic agent," and a "teacher" is to be in specific ways a servant, and to be a servant will require real self-understanding by the pastor.— (16,114)

. . . It is not a sign of a redemptive fellowship when a pastor regularly and faithfully calls on the sick, the shut-in, and the aged. This merely indicates that a church has hired a minister who, because he wants to or because he is paid to, visits such persons. The programs the pastor promotes should be programs in which other members of the congregation visit the sick, the aged, and the shut-in.—(16,137)

. . . My pastor is an equipper. Consequently, our laymen are involved in Lay Renewal and the Lay WIN School of Evangelism. Many people come to know Christ each week through the witness of our lay people. They are involved in various types of ministry which result in an exciting service to others. That's the only way. That's the New Testament way.— Lamar Slay, First Baptist Church, Pasadena, Texas.

. . . When a pastor sees his role as the preparer of and pray-er for his people, it makes a difference in how he preaches. He begins to see Sunday not as a climax for the week just past, but a day of preparation for the week to come.—(**8,**47)

. . . When a pastor sees his primary role as a preparer of his people, it makes a difference in how he prays. He will stop praying for nebulous "revival" among his people and start praying for *persons* who, as Bruce Larson put it, will "dare to live now." He will stop praying for emotional responses from his people and start praying for effective inroads by them. He will stop praying for *more members* and start praying for *more ministers* and, thereby, get both!—(**8,**46)

. . . Those on the front lines in the major spiritual and moral struggles of our time are undoubtedly the lay people, but the lay people are not likely to make an effective witness unless they are guided, instructed, and inspired by those engaged in a vital ministry. Whenever we discover something new and exciting in the church we always find that, in the midst of it, there is a *man*. It is men who make the difference and some of the men who are most effective in our total civilization are those whose lives are dedicated to the public or professional ministry. The Christian ideal is that of the universal or lay ministry, but this ideal cannot be realized unless there are men who specialize in making it real.—(**16,**7)

. . . The "seekers" merit the special attention of the equipping minister. True, a minister must be pastor of all the congregation, both the interested and those who couldn't care less, but to get help in the cause of the church he will necessarily have to tell his story to those who will listen—and help. Jesus Christ did not reach everyone, and while he occasionally appeared before large groups, the vast bulk of his time was spent with the twelve. To *think* that failure is indicated by a lack of numbers is the real failure, not the fact of the small numerical response itself. Numerical success is a by-product, not a goal.—(**16,**137)

EVANGELISM, LIFE-STYLE

. . . Our goal is to *find the hole in the Outsider's heart*. Nothing is any more important for a significant relationship than to find that hole! It can be a problem—a mother with a teenage boy who is breaking her heart, a husband with a wife who is about to leave him, a man whose business is about to go bankrupt, or the couple who just discovered their little boy has cancer. Sooner or later everyone will have a gaping hole in his heart, and through that hole the good news of Jesus Christ can be shared as the power of God for salvation.—(**19,**94)

. . . Gabriel Marcel described it with these words: "I am obliged to bear witness because I hold, as it were, a particle of light; and to keep it to myself would be equivalent to extinguishing it."—(**19**,130)

. . . Christian faith suffers violence not from lack of power, but from lack of *exposure.*—(**19**,113)

. . . Carroll Ray, Jr. was saved in a Renewal Weekend at the First Baptist Church, Burleson, Texas. After that God placed a desire in his heart to share Christ at work, home, and wherever he went.

He says, "Rather than look for people to witness to I began to ask the Lord who he was already dealing with among my friends and business associates. First, there was a vice-president of a large corporation. Then there was the drug addict and others. Jesus talked to people along the way. His example is the one I like to follow." Since that time God has revealed a steady stream of people searching for him and reality.

. . . Remember, evangelism is *one hungry beggar telling another hungry beggar where to find bread.*—(**19**,95)

. . . A second advantage held by the lay minister . . . is that he is often closer to common life. He is already in the factory, the bank or the office, and thus does not need to gain entrance from the outside. The insider, with his amateur standing, has a great opportunity because of his daily contacts in the course of his ordinary duties.—(**25**,41-42)

. . . The nonwitnessing Christian is a contradiction in terms.—(**8**,143)

. . . Those who witness should realize the following points: (1) Nearly everything a person does is based upon how he truly feels about himself. (2) Effective sharing of the gospel depends on the Holy Spirit, not YOU! (3) Every Outsider is interested in himself, not Jesus. (4) Learn to love the Outsider for what he will become. (5) Recognize the Outsider's virtues. (6) Overlook his faults! (7) Be sensitive to the other's needs at all times. (8) Be a helping hand, but don't smother. (9) Allow time for the Holy Spirit to do his work. (10) Be transparently OPEN—so that Christ can reveal himself through you.—(**19**,117-119)

. . . A healthy body is necessary to do effective work. To attempt evangelism while the body of Christ is sick and ailing is worse than useless. It is not difficult to keep a body of Christians healthy and vital if the individuals involved (especially leaders) are concerned to bear one another's burdens, confess their faults one to another, and to instruct and admonish one another in love, by means of the Word of God. It is by these means that the church is becoming what its Lord desires.—(22,114)

. . . The cure of souls must be practiced on a one-to-one basis. Imagine, if you will, a Christian doctor who steps into his crowded waiting room and asks, "Who wants to be healed?" and then proceeds to tell all who respond, "Well, the work is finished. Christ has died to make you well. Go in health and peace." The absurdity of this is obvious. He must see the patients one by one. As he works with them, he becomes a prism through which the healing power of Christ can touch each one in a different way. Certainly healing is the work of Christ on the cross, but it must be channeled or transmitted person to person, even as in medical healing.—(12,108)

. . . When I was sixty years of age God saved me and gave me a compulsion to witness. I was trying to reach as many of my old drinking buddies as possible. One evening my wife, Helen, and I visited the home of a man with whom I used to work and drink. We spent an enjoyable time telling them how wonderful it was to be a Christian, and as we were getting ready to leave, his wife asked me if I ever visited hospitals to minister to the sick. I had just finished building myself into an image of a proper Christian so I couldn't very well tell her that I never had; in fact, I had never given that phase of ministry a thought, so I lied and said yes.

She said that in the nursing home where her mother was, a nineteen-year-old boy named Larry was a patient. She said that he had told her that he didn't believe that there was a God, for if there were he wouldn't be as he was while other people were normal. I promised to go see him, and we left. I had intended to go home and forget it, but God wouldn't let me. During the next week, I tried in vain to get others to go and see him. The following Friday when I stopped for the traffic light near the home, I couldn't get my foot on the gas pedal when the light changed. A voice kept saying, "Go to see Larry." By this time the cars behind were honking their horns so I said, "OK, Lord, I'll go," and immediately I was able to continue. When I found Larry, another patient was reading to him. He was sitting in a wheelchair and I was shocked when I saw him. He had a normal head attached to a glob of what passed for a body. He was unable to move anything except his eyes and mouth. He weighed only forty-five pounds.

I was very uncomfortable but went directly to him and said, "Hello, Larry, I'm Carl. I don't know why but God sent me to see you." He replied, "Where is God?" The only answer that I could think of was, "I found him when I met his Son, Jesus Christ." Well, we talked for a few minutes, and I read him some Scripture, then I said I had another appointment and had to go. I wanted to get out of there in the worst way. As I was leaving Larry said, "Will you come back and see me?" I said, "Yes," and left. When I got to my car, I cried so hard that it was several minutes before I was able to drive.

During the following weekend, I was more miserable than I had ever been before in all of my life. I knew that God wanted me to do something about Larry, but I didn't know what or how. Everyone that I contacted in the church told me to pray and God would give me the answer. Well, I prayed and prayed, but received no answer.

On Monday night at bedtime I told Helen I was going to pray all night if necessary to learn the will of God. She went to sleep immediately. We sleep in twin beds, so I sat on mine and prayed aloud, bareing my heart to God. No answer. Finally I stopped trying to pray and really talked to God as if he were in the room with me. I told him he had put me through hell for the last few days and that I had had it. I said, "If you'll tell me what to do I'll do it, but if you don't I'll never see that boy again. I just can't stand this turmoil inside me." All thoughts left my mind and I heard a clear voice say, "Have your Bible class pray for Larry tomorrow night. Have your church pray for Larry Wednesday night. Have the church that meets in Jack Musselman's house pray for Larry." The voice stopped and I said, "That's easy, what else?" He said, "Go to sleep."

I proceeded to follow all of the instructions that God had given me and went to see Larry on the following Friday. I told him what had happened, that I knew where God was now, and if he would let me I would try to show him. After that I visited Larry every Friday and spent two hours each time with him. Out of these visits a great love grew between us. He paid me the greatest compliment I had ever received one day when he said, "Carl, you really love me don't you?" I said, "Of course, why do you ask?" Larry replied, "There are a lot of people who come into this place and sing songs and all that stuff, but they're just do-gooders; they don't really love me, but you do." This gave me the opportunity to explain to him that it wasn't me but Christ who lived in me that really loved him.

A few visits later Larry asked me how he could get to know Jesus like I did, and I had the joy of watching him receive Lord Jesus as his personal Savior. Later he told me that as he was now a member of the body of Christ, he would like to be baptized and join my church. I made the arrangements and took him to my church. When the invitation was given, I pushed him down the aisle to make his public profession of faith. I gave the church our testimony to date, and the pastor set the date for his baptism two weeks later.

The following weekend, I was engaged in a Lay Renewal Mission in a church in Pahokee, Florida. During the noon luncheon on Saturday I received a phone call from my pastor informing me that Larry had passed away at three o'clock that morning. He never was formally baptized but Larry is waiting to greet me when I come home.—Carl Beers of Laymen's Landing, Deerfield Beach, Florida.

FELLOWSHIP

. . . We smile, sometimes at the church supper, but we are not wise when we do so. It is the oldest Christian ritual.—(23,71)

. . . One church, Broadway Baptist in Kansas City, has dared to believe that the church's primary function is not mission but fellowship. It believes that Christ called into being by the power of the Holy Spirit, a fellowship of people who could learn to care deeply for one another. This church does exactly that. The pastor visits with no more than twelve to eighteen people each week. (They are the same twelve to eighteen people each week!) These people in turn begin to care for others in groups of twelve to eighteen, who in turn care for others. The pastor makes almost no house calls or hospital calls but leaves the ministry of caring for one another to members of his church. They are not only reaching out and touching the lives of many people on the outside, they are discovering a new kind of life and caring on the inside.—(12,108)

FORGIVENESS

. . . Some people forgive after the manner of a lemon squeezer. When the last drop of juice by way of apology, explanation, atonement, and repentance has been squeezed out, a reluctant forgiveness is offered, but often offered in such a way that the offending one feels even worse than before. Many people do not seem to know what real forgiveness is.

GIFTS OF THE SPIRIT

. . . A pastor friend of mine once came to me in frustration. He knew that my pastoral relationship to my congregation focused upon "turning loose" those with gifts to conduct their ministries. He said, "How do you safe-guard the congregation from the self-appointed 'teacher' who can't *teach*, or the self-appointed 'leader' who has a penchant for making everyone upset by his highhanded methods?" The answer is quite clear: spiritual gifts are *service gifts,* and they are to be used for the good of the Body. This means that they are to be exercised when the Body accepts them as good. Group affirmation of spiritual gifts is the most important way to insure the individual member of the Body doesn't end up proudly "doing his own thing!"—(**17**,55)

. . . The gifts of the Spirit require us to live interdependently serving in the corporate life of the Body . . . not as *Lone Rangers.*—(**17**,57)

. . . Do you want to discover your gifts? Set out to relate to the sick lives of Outsiders in your area. All the gifts for "healing" you will need will be discovered in the journey of life-style evangelism. All the areas you need to learn about will emerge from your actual involvement in ministry.
    It's like learning to ride a bicycle! You'll never get the hang of it by watching training films and reading books on the subject. You must actually ride one. As you do, your skills of steering, pedaling, balancing, etc., will be called forth.—(**17**,30)

. . . Too often we wonder how our gifts can be *discovered,* when we ought to be wondering where our lives can be *used.*—(**17**,23)

. . . To have a greater encounter with God and to come away enamored with the experience rather than with God is sophisticated adultery. We are not to magnify the gift instead of the giver. We are not to go out as an evangel for our gifts, but we are to go out as an evangel for God.— (**18**,105)

. . . One who has the gift of faith believes that even the impossible can be achieved. One pastor, upon emerging from a boring and uninspiring session of his board, commented that if "our church is ever going to get anywhere, we should have at least one person on the board who is totally insane."—(**16**,78)

. . . Some years ago, a Christian family moved next door to a couple who were not *only* Outsiders, but also violently anti-church. They spared no pains in flaunting their vulgar way before the "religious fanatics" next door. Then the Outsider husband contracted an anemia which caused him to spend days at a time in bed. Previously, Sundays had been spent manicuring his lawn—now, the grass grew high. Because of financial problems which developed as a result of the breadwinner's illness, eventually even the cost of hiring a boy to mow the lawn was out of reach.

Early one Saturday morning, the Outsiders awoke to the humming sound of an electric lawnmower in their yard. The entire family next door was at work, trimming the hedges, digging up beds, edging around the sidewalk. For weeks, the routine continued. Knowing the prejudice of the Outsiders no verbal statements were made by the Christian couple.

You know what happened! In time, their ministry of love broke down the prejudice. Opportunity for dialogue followed. . . . This family exhibited the gift of service.—(17,42-43)

. . . One of those *gifts* is that of "pastor." It is his function to "equip the saints for the work of the ministry" (Eph. 4:11-12). It is not his function to do the ministry *for* them; rather, he is to equip the people for their ministries. Thus, the distinction between clergy and laity is not one of *position* as much as one of *function*. The underlying truth is that *each* member of the body of Christ has a particular ministry. Being a pastor is but one of them. He is the "equipping" minister.—(9,55-56)

. . . Every Christian's gift must be exercised in the energy of the Holy Spirit if it is to be effective. There are several steps to using one's gift in the energy of the Spirit. (1) In prayer ask God to cleanse your life and to use you in the Spirit's power. (2) Yield to God's will (Rom. 6:16; 12:1,2). (3) Be filled with the Holy Spirit (Eph. 5:18). Allow the Holy Spirit of God to permeate every part of you. Turn your every decision over to the Spirit's control. Commitment to His control is the key.—(15,141)

. . . A manufacturer had spent thousands of dollars in efforts to repair a heavy-duty electric motor that was always breaking down. He finally called in an expert, who tapped the motor twice with a hammer; it started instantly and ran smoothly and efficiently. When the expert sent in a bill for $50.00 the manufacturer, in a rage, demanded an itemized bill. That was just too much for two taps of a hammer!

The bill came as follows:	Tapping with hammer	$ 1.00
	Knowing where to tap	49.00
		$50.00

It isn't enough to know about religion or the religious field; unless we know how to put that knowledge to work—unless we use our spiritual gifts in a practical way—of what use is our knowledge?

. . . Often the church recognizes the gifts which have been bestowed upon fellow members. From the beginning of the church, some of the "spirituals" have been discovered only through being in proper fellowship with the body.

A little known detail in the life of the great Dr. George W. Truett illustrates this perfectly. Converted at the age of nineteen, he followed his parents from Georgia to Whitewright, Texas. At age twenty-three, he attended the formal business meeting of his church, the Whitewright Baptist Church. After a season of prayer, the various members of the congregation stood to their feet to share a common insight given them concerning young Truett. One man said, "The Lord has given me a burden for George. I must share with you my conviction that he is being called to preach." Others acknowledged that, during the season of prayer, the Lord had affirmed the same truth in their hearts. All eyes turned to the young man in question . . .

George W. Truett stood to his feet, deeply moved. He confessed he had felt no such call of God in his own heart. He also indicated that he considered it mandatory to be obedient to what God was calling him to do through the word given to the Body.

That night, George W. Truett was ordained as a preacher of the gospel!—(18,88-89)

HAPPINESS

. . . The time to be happy is now;
The place to be happy is here;
The way to be happy is to make other people happy.—(14,85)

HONESTY

. . . Christ wants his church to be unshockable, democratic, permissive, and filled with the real Spirit—a fellowship where people can come in and say, "I'm sunk!" "I'm beat!" "I've had it!" What keeps us from this quality of life? Many church members are genuinely committed to Jesus Christ but have no resulting power. The rebirth of a biblical theology in most major denominations today has resulted in a commitment-centered message. I genuinely rejoice in it, but it's not enough. One more altar call, decision card, church officers' retreat, or camp fire surrender won't do it. Something else is needed. *A fellowship must exist where committed people can begin to be honest with each other and discover the dimension of apostolic fellowship.*—(11,21)

. . . Jesus did not practice secrecy about Himself. The only way we could know about His temptations in the wilderness is that He must have told His disciples, for no one else was there with Him.—(13,47)

. . . A Christian is most truly a Christian when he is most truly himself.— (14,85)

. . . Last summer my older son, Peter, had the privilege of spending ten days at a Young Life ranch. When he returned, I met his bus and immediately noticed a difference in this "typical" adolescent boy. He was outside himself, communicative, sensitive, and excited.

As we drove home, the first thing Peter said gave me the clue not only to what had happened but to how it had happened. "Dad," he said, "I became a Christian at the ranch last week. It's strange: I didn't learn a thing about Jesus that I didn't know before I went there. But I met some people who were *real.*"—(14,19-20)

. . . We must acknowledge that the church is for losers. The church is not for those who "have it made" or for those who are an entrenched part of the "establishment," however you choose to identify or interpret the establishment. Yes, the church is for the dispossessed and for those who can honestly say that they do not have it made.—(14,25)

JOURNEY

. . . I have learned to say: "Lord here I am; use me as you would like." Then I take a deep breath, lean back, and get ready for an exciting ride. The Lord has used and is now using the Lay Renewal Movement. When people get together to praise the Lord and share their lives, love, and testimonies with others with no thought of praise or reward for themselves; God takes control. When he is in control things happen. This is a most exciting life.—Billy B. Hale, Mullin, Texas.

LAITY

. . . A lot of laymen are like wheelbarrows—not good unless pushed. Some are like canoes—they need to be paddled. Some are like kites—if you don't keep a string on them they fly away. Some are like a good watch— open face, pure gold, quietly busy, and full of good works. Which one are you?

. . . If you are a baptized Christian, you are already a minister. Whether you are ordained or not is immaterial. No matter how you react, the statement remains true. You may be surprised, alarmed, pleased, antagonized, suspicious, acquiescent, scornful, or enraged. Nevertheless, you are a minister of Christ.—(1)

. . . When I was a pastor I found myself either in the office studying, counseling, or administrating church business. It dawned on me that the layman's principal value stems from his numerical strength. He is found in every church and community, at all economic and social levels. He has access to all the places where men are in need of the church and its message. He is in the banks and factories, traveling on the highways and airlines, working at civilian and military assignments. Through the sheer breadth of these contacts, numbered in the uncounted millions, he has access to far more human beings than I alone could ever reach. And he meets these people where they live. His potential as a witness is enormous.—(3,63-64)

. . . The traditional approach to the ministry of the church has viewed the pastor as the one who performs the ministry and the people as those who support the work. The discovery of the laity as the church's greatest resource for the ministry is the greatest discovery of this day. These churches which have decided that they really want to do something for God and for the people have discovered talent, interest, and a commitment far beyond their expectation. *The hope of the ministering church is the informed, inspired, committed layman.*—(4,97)

LAY MINISTRY

. . . The key word on the lips of those who are concerned for the world is *involvement*. We must be involved in the struggles, hopes, fears, needs of the world. This means politically involved, socially involved, psychologically involved. The fact that we belong to Christ does not excuse us from our responsibility to minister to the world's needs in these various areas. In fact, as Christians, we should be especially sensitive to the tasks and problems at hand and particularly concerned to do our part in meeting needs and solving problems.—(14,125)

LAY PREACHING

. . . When I am gone on a Sunday morning, the chances are good that one of our laymen will preach. In the last three years, twenty of our own laymen have preached on Sunday morning. During the last calendar year, eight laymen preached. . . . Our laymen preach the Sundays when I am on vacation in the summer. . . . (These people) discover that they are meant to be ministers of Christ, like the lay people described in the New Testament. When a layman speaks of his own pilgrimage before the congregation, the people listen and take heed as they seldom do when a professional clergyman says the same things.—(20,78-79)

. . . Amateur preaching wins by its freshness, but very often, if continued, apes the very ministry it replaces. A great deal more is involved in discovering what it means to be a layman in the church in this day.—(4,10)

LAY RENEWAL TEAMS

. . . A gifted pastor in South Dakota is much in demand as a speaker and evangelist. But he has discovered that teams of his own laymen going into other churches to witness are more effective in reaching people and aiding in renewal. These teams of laymen are not a schedule-stretcher for a busy person, but actually a more generous and effective means of one church sharing its "new life" with other churches.—(13,87)

LISTENING

. . . I know that you believe you understand what you think I said, but, I am not sure you realize that what you heard is not what I meant.

. . . Psychologists say it is impossible to distinguish intense listening from love.—(13,90)

LONELINESS

. . . It doesn't matter how many friends one has. There's no escape from loneliness. You wonder what would happen to those friends if the circumstances of your life would change—if you would lose the qualities other people found desirable. Friends are perhaps the greatest thing God can give you, outside of the gift of Himself, but even with friends one has deep loneliness. . . . The mark of a Christian is that he knows how to deal with his loneliness.—(14,100)

LORDSHIP

. . . Is it possible to be a Christian and to be active in all the programs of a Southern Baptist church for over twenty-five years and then be awakened one day to the realization that all you have done those years were only stubble in the eyes of God? It is possible, and that very thing happened to me.

Through my school years, college, and military service, I tried my best to live as I thought a Christian should. When my wife and I started civilian life after World War II, we were very active in our church. Because of my initiative it was easy to become involved in every phase of leadership in my church. As we reared our four children, I led the Sunday School, directed the music, and did many other things in the church. I enjoyed my service so much I was at the church more than I was at home. I know now that I neglected my family many times to perform some church service. In spite of my failings, God was so gracious that he took care of the spiritual welfare of our children. He gave them a love for Christ and his church that has remained.

In March, 1973, our church had a Lay Renewal Weekend. On Friday evening in the small group activity, I had an opportunity to examine my own life. I was not pleased with what I saw. Through this experience I realized that all the service I had been doing for the Lord was done in my own strength. I made the decision that weekend to let Jesus Christ have control of every phase of my life. It has not been easy. Each day I have to come to God to confess my failures and ask him to forgive me and to fill me again and live through me to do what needs to be done. God has honored this commitment. Before, my Bible study was strictly for teaching the other person, to supply in a pulpit, or to give a devotional. Since that experience, my Bible study has been for the purpose of searching the Scriptures to see what God has to say to me in the area of my own relationship to him.

He has opened the door for me to serve as a coordinator in Lay Renewal Weekends. This is a new approach in our denomination that is helping the lay person to see that God wants a life surrendered to him for the purpose of sharing with others—not just to be a part of a program.

Now there is a difference in my attitude. My life is full of joy and peace that comes from Jesus Christ.—Joe Herndon, Duncan, Oklahoma

. . . The Bible speaks about having the mind of Christ. You invite another person to live inside of you when you yield a part of yourself to him and make room for him at the center. This Person then has a plan for your life and begins to supply new direction, new resources, new strengths.—(12,28)

. . . Men cannot feel the touch of His spirit to make them something they are not unless they will respond to His invitation to follow Him. His continuing invitation is, "Follow me and I will make you fishers of men." He says, "I will use every talent and all the training you have, but I will transpose it so it will be used for spiritual ends. In the deepest sense I will make you what you are not."—(3,90)

LOVE

. . . A man told me recently that his life was changed when his pastor asked him, "Whom do you love?" He replied, "Well, I love everybody." "No," the pastor pursued. "Whom do you really love right now?" "Well," he said, "I don't have any enemies." But his pastor persisted, "I'm not asking you that. I'm asking you to tell me one person specifically by name that you are now involved in loving in a particular way." Well, the fact that this man could think of no one led to a genuine change in his own life. He discovered that it takes a new dimension of commitment to love one person specifically rather than to love all humanity generally and to have no enemies.—(**12,**65)

. . . To love at all is to be vulnerable. Love anything, and your heart will certainly be wrung and possibly broken. If you want to make sure of keeping it intact, you must give your heart to no one. Wrap it carefully round with hobbies and little luxuries; avoid all entanglements; lock it up safe in the coffin of your selfishness.—(**17,**81)

MINISTRY

. . . Can you visualize a membership who considered themselves as *all* being a part of the working crew with no passenger list? Each is seeking his ministry and many have found it. They turn to the pastor to enlist his help in sharpening their skills for *their* ministries. Groups are clustered here and there around tasks and functions and ministries. Some are in the ghetto, some among the hippies, others among the doctors and the lawyers. Some are involved in physical and economic assistance, others are in direct spiritual ministries—but all of the tasks are infused with the Christ-message. *Can you imagine?*—(**10,**34)

. . . A wise man once said that every Christian needs two conversions: one out of the world and a second back into the world.—(**14,**115)

. . . The body of Christ is the body of my brother and sister. I honor Christ when I honor them, and I disgrace Christ when I do not assume a personal responsibility and concern for them.—(**18,**93)

. . . Nicholas Murray Butler says, "I divide the world into three classes— the few who make things happen; the many who watch things happen; and the overwhelming majority who have no notion of what happens."— (**13,**66)

. . . While we have not yet fully defined the lay ministry, it is obvious that it has nothing to do with "chores about the church"! So many of us are like the pastor who, when asked what he would do if forty or fifty men approached him after a service requesting something to do, replied: "I don't know what it could be; we already have sixty ushers!" Whatever it is, it is not that!

NEW AUTHORITY

. . . Each era has demanded a different center of authority through which God could confront the world. In the Dark Ages, God used the very structure of the Church as the one organized, learned institution in a chaotic society. During the Reformation the Bible was rediscovered and became for Western civilization the center of authority through which God spoke. Still later, preaching became God's primary means of confronting men.

But the world today is not impressed by the Bible, or by the church, or by preaching. And we cannot confront a needy world with God's love primarily by these means. The climate of our time is one in which people listen most readily to laymen with whom they can identify. So as in the first century, ordinary laymen have become the center of spiritual authority.

Madison Avenue is discovering that the person down the street who is "just like me" is the person I will listen to. Much of our present-day advertising focuses on unknown women in laundromats, unknown truck drivers, or unknown students reporting the findings of dental tests.—(13,86)

NEW CONVERTS

. . . It's important to wrap loving arms of fellowship around the baby Christian. After all, he'll probably lose all his old friends within the first three months he is a Christian. If you don't include him in your social gatherings, where will he go for activity and sharing?—(17,88)

. . . Conversion is that experience that makes all the difference. It explains the incongruity of the brilliant surgeon who commits suicide because his life has become dull, while a penniless ex-alcoholic and chronic invalid finds meaning every day in a veterans hospital. One is so bored he takes his life; the other is so contagious that others find faith and help through a relationship with him.—(12,26)

. . . I was born into a family of liberal church people who never attended church, except on special occasions such as Easter or a funeral. Until my adult years, I never knew the meaning of God's love, never learned about

Jesus, and never experienced the power and presence of the Holy Spirit. Not having been "raised up" in the way of the Lord, it came as quite a surprise when, as a twelve-year-old boy, I came home one Thursday night to find with my mother and father the Sunday School superintendent from the church where they held membership. They told me that they had decided it was time for me to join the church, and they even cued me on when to go down to the front of the church as the "invitation" was given. I was confused and bewildered as to the meaning of all this.

That night, as I lay in bed, a terrible blackness came over my soul. I tossed and turned all night, caught up in the agony and fear that flooded my being. I didn't realize it then, but now I know that it was the Holy Spirit burdening my heart and causing me to be afraid to the point of rebellion against "going down" to the front of the church on Sunday. This blackness of soul lasted on to Sunday. Finally when that day came, I refused to go to church. I resisted all threats and pleading. Never again would I attend that church, and I never told my parents of my experience with the "blackness."

From the age of twelve until I came to know Jesus as Savior at the age of thirty-two, I wandered through life searching for some rhyme and reason to it all. I tested and tasted all the world could offer. I became thoroughly involved in and totally encrusted with sin. A few years in the military helped to further harden my heart, and I reached a point of being without compassion or concern for anyone. The only stabilizing factor in my life was my beautiful and wonderful wife whom God had given me and who eventually would share the glorious experience of Jesus with me. I was a classic type considered beyond hope by those Christians who tried to witness to me. Many times the effort was made to share Christ with me by concerned Christians. The result was always the same—I taunted them, argued against their beliefs, often embarrassed them with my language, and never failed to frustrate them with my unreachable spirit.

In truth their prayers for me and efforts of concern were being heard and God was really at work in my heart all the while. Each effort made, each word spoken, and each act of kindness left a seed. Fruition was not to be realized until many years later. Just when the turning point came I cannot say. Each time I met with worldly success there followed failure. Each time I settled down to enjoy life, there came unhappiness and dissatisfaction. I began to think there must be something more to life than what I had found. Finally came a day when I was alone at home and a hunger in my soul was not to be denied. I asked God—whom I didn't know and whom I must have grieved—to help me find him. I didn't even know how to ask, but praise his name, he understood and the seed of the first miracle was planted.

A few days later our small daughter was standing in the car seat beside me as we passed the James Avenue Baptist Church located near my home on the south side of Fort Worth. My daughter became the instrument of God's will as she said, "Daddy, let's go to church there someday." A feeling of spiritual need and hunger came over me in that moment. Since my wife and I never discussed spiritual things, I was unaware of her own search for God. After I told her of that comment, we readily agreed to go the next Sunday. Church time came and the sermon was delivered by the pastor. When the invitation was given, with thirsty souls, my wife and I rushed down the aisle to claim Jesus as Lord and Savior. Oh, glorious day! The change was instant and complete. I wanted to shout it to the world and share my Jesus with everyone. I went home from that experience and poured all the liquor down the drain, dumped my beer stock in the garbage, and tossed all my cigarettes away. Anything that was alien to God had to go. My language was different and my hardened attitudes were changed to concern, love, and compassion. I was filled with an urgency to share Jesus with the world.

From the day of my salvation, God has blessed me so wonderfully with his love. He continues to reveal more of Jesus to me, and he makes me aware of his presence through the Holy Spirit. I have known good times and bad, hardship and ease, with every experience strengthening me to face life in the freshness of his love and purpose. He allows me to share his love with others. I have been given places of service in his ministry and have been privileged to know and experience the sweetness of Christian fellowship. If a sinful reprobate like me can be saved and changed and used in his kingdom, then millions of others can be, too! Spread the word, plant the seed, God will give the harvest.

I would not trade one single second of my time with Christ for all of the years of sin without him.—Damon Brown, Atlanta, Georgia

OUTSIDERS

. . . People on the outside need to know that people on the inside care about them, not just about their pledge or their initial commitment but about the whole shape of their life. Even more elementary, people outside need to know that people inside are genuinely glad to see them.—(12,109)

PASTORS

. . . Renewal will not come to pass unless someone works at it, and pastors are the ones who are most free to give themselves to this holy task. This is the equipping ministry.—(10,12)

PRAYER

. . . When I was a student at college, my BSU director made a profound statement. She said, "When you need to pray most is when you don't feel like praying. When you need to read the Bible most is when you don't feel like reading the Bible."

. . . Keep your prayer honest. There is a great deal of pretense and sham in the best of us. We do not present all of ourselves to anyone. We usually reveal only a part of ourselves for fear that people will not love us if they know all about us. Unfortunately we carry this masquerade into our prayer life. Somehow we forget that the very essence of the good news of God is that he knows exactly what we are like. We are naked before him. All sham is gone. All pretense is gone. In spite of this, he still loves us and cares for us. A part of man's ability to be honest with life can begin in his prayer life when he is honest with God. Probably the only place where we are able to be completely ourselves and to feel at home is in the presence of God.—(4,62)

. . . Stripped of all its theological encumbrances, *prayer* means to *talk with God*. Thus, to use the expression, "Say your prayers," is to miss the mark. Merely to recite to God is to talk *at* him, not *to* and *with* him. Yet, as simple as this may sound, it is one of the major hurdles in the journey of the Christian life. Few ever cross it. Those who do are those who make the transition from *recitation* to *relationship*.—(9,33)

. . . It was said of the saintly Uncle John Vassar that one evening some friends secreted themselves outside the window of his room to find how long he prayed before he went to bed at night. To their surprise Uncle John put on his night clothing and climbed promptly into bed. The friends were disappointed and perplexed. They had taken for granted that he would spend considerable time on his knees before retiring. But the old saint just got into bed, pulled the covers up around his neck, and then quietly said, "Good night, Lord Jesus, I have had a wonderful time with you today, and look forward to spending another one tomorrow if you see fit to spare me." Uncle John Vassar had got beyond the mere stage of petition, of just asking and requesting. He had come to the place of sweet, sustained communion and fellowship with his Lord and Savior.—(5,23)

. . . A prayer group can be as much an escape from the real issues of life as a cocktail party. Jesus may be calling us to face certain facts, or to make right certain relationships, while we escape him and his demands by busying ourselves with a cozy group of Christians who enjoy being together, praying for the world.—(**13**,73)

. . . However, a prayer group can be the most relevant, vital, powerful, and up-to-date appointment we keep all week. Through a prayer group that is open to God, lives can be changed and the whole course of human events altered. That this has happened many times in the past is history. There is no magic in just praying. Prayer doesn't change things. God changes things.—(**13**,73-74)

. . . During a preaching mission, a woman asked me to visit her home. When I entered, I found her looking out the window, holding the lace curtains open with both hands. She called me to look out with her and said, "In *that* house lives a couple I have known only passingly. And in the one beside it is an alcoholic I have not spoken to for five years. To my left, a family I have never known to go to church. To my right, an unknown young couple with a new baby and a penchant for wild parties."

The curtains dropped as she buried her face in her hands and wept. She continued, "Do you know that in my entire adult life I have never even *prayed* for the salvation of anyone except my own two daughters?"—(**17**,82)

. . . There are several areas of daily prayer that should be evident in each life: (1) Prayer of praise. Tell God you love him. Praise him for at least one of his characteristics: his goodness, patience, mercy, greatness, love, holiness, understanding, strength, availability. (2) Prayer of thanksgiving. Thank God for one specific thing in each of the following areas for which you are thankful this day. Tell him that you are thankful for material blessings such as house, car, shoes, heat; physical blessings—mind, eyes, health, hands; people—one specific person; and spiritual blessings—salvation, prayer, love, joy and peace. (3) Prayer of confession. We should search our hearts and confess to God all known sins! Remember, confession is agreeing with God that what you did was wrong; being genuinely sorry for your sins; willing to turn from your sins and repent; and being grateful that God has cleansed you and restored you to his fellowship. Confess sins of tongue—things that we said which were wrong, unkind, dirty; sins of action—things we did that broke God's laws and hurt others; sins of thought—the thoughts we allowed to stay in our minds that were wrong; and sins of omission—things that we should have done or said but omitted. (4) Prayer of intercession. Pray for specific blessings for specific people such as a member of the family, missionary, a pastor and Sunday School teacher, a Christian friend, an unsaved friend, a political leader, and others who are on your heart. (5) Prayer of petition. Here we ask God about any and everything that we have on our hearts. List them—and when answered, erase and thank God. (6) Prayer of silence. Pause for a few seconds and listen to see if God wants to speak to you. When you believe God has spoken, write it down, if necessary, to keep from forgetting.

QUIET TIME

. . . Sometimes as long as a weekend, sometimes as short as an afternoon, the earnest follower is constantly in need of getting away from all voices save the Voice.—(8,82)

. . . In 1882 at Cambridge University, the world was first given the slogan: "Remember the Morning Watch." Enthusiasm and activity were the order of the day—days were filled up with lectures, games, and bull sessions. But these Christian men saw their need to spend time with God. They looked for an answer—the morning watch. The plan: to spend the first minutes of the day with God in prayer and Bible reading.

The idea caught fire—the campus got turned on to the Lord, and resulted in the famous Cambridge 7—a band of prominent athletes, wealthy and educated, who gave up everything to go to China for Christ—the first missionary movement.

It wasn't easy. In fact, they had a hard time getting out of bed. A fellow named Thornton was determined to be disciplined. He invented a fool-proof cure for his laziness. He had a contraption set up by his bed in which the vibration of the alarm clock set a fishing rod in motion and his sheets, hooked by the fishing line, moved into the air off the sleeper's body.

This guy was determined to get up. You must want to meet God that badly, too.—Barry St. Clair, unpublished article entitled "Time Alone with God"

. . . Vance Havner says that when Jesus said, "Come ye apart and rest awhile," He really meant: "Come ye apart and rest awhile—*or come ye apart!*"—(8,100)

. . . We, indeed, still have a little piety; we say a few hasty prayers; we sing meaningfully a few hymns; we read snatches from the Bible. But all of this is far removed from the massive dose that we sorely need if we are to be the men and women who can perform a healing service in our generation.—(24,86-87)

RELATIONSHIPS

. . . When we are able to appropriate and develop such qualities as openness, transparency, and lack of deviousness, we find that life is enhanced both in terms of our sense of well-being and in terms of our relationships with others. When we lack these qualities, we not only fail to live up to our full potential but also run the risk of damaging those we love.—(14,101-102)

RENEWAL

. . . *Renewal*—a word for a journey, a journey of commitment, a commitment to "Christ in you, the hope of Glory" (Col. 1:27). Renewal has strengthened my personal life as a pastor in freedom of leadership both in organization and worship. Renewal has helped me to better be "all things to all men." Renewal has brought my church alive. Prayer meeting attendance has grown 50 percent, "Witnessing as you go" has become a practice, a reality, not just a statement. Renewal—there are not words to tell you what God is doing in so many of my people. People have opened up, freed up, and confessed up.

As a pastor, I thank God for the truth of God's Word shared in renewal that leads to fantastic experiences in Jesus. This is the way it should be—from truth to experience. "Renewal" is helping the saved to "walk."—Roy Jerrell, pastor, Mount Vernon, Missouri

. . . There is a dangerous tendency in some forms of renewal which would replace corporate worship with dialogue, sharing times, and small-group study. While these are both needed and valid for renewal, they are not substitutes for worship. Many have wisely begun to employ these methods in an effort to revitalize the Sunday night service and give it meaning! Some, however, would wrongly replace all worship with such. There must be a time and a place when God is given *his say,* or we shall lose something unique to corporate worship.—(8,79)

RESTITUTION

. . . One day I prayed Psalm 139:23-24, where it says, "Search me, O God," and he did! He began to show me the sin in my life. I was in our egg house where we process our eggs to get them ready for market. We have egg separating machines to do this. Before we can begin, the machine must be filled with water and all moving parts oiled. I was doing this when the impression came to my mind in the form of a question.

"Where did you get that oil can?" Immediately I knew. I had conveniently forgotten for ten years where I got it. I considered it my oil can. But, I knew. I had stolen that oil can from a plant I worked in while in college. Right then I said, "Yes, Lord, I know where I got it, I stole it. I'm sorry please forgive me." I thought that would be the end of it. It wasn't. He said (to my mind) "I want you to take it back!" I thought, who would ever miss it or even know it was gone after this length of time. I said I would. I also said, "Lord, you forgot about that electric drill I stole at about the same time. I'll take them both back." When time came to take them back, I cleaned them up and put them in a sack and went back to the plant of my former employment. I was hoping all the way that the plant manger of ten years ago would be gone. He was still there and worst of all he remembered me well. We talked. I finally told him why I was there. There was no electrifying response from the manager. We simply said good-bye. On the way home I felt clean. It was a cleanliness I want to keep regardless of how many oil cans I have to return.—Charles Boyd gave this earthy testimony about restitution of sin.

SERVICE

. . . If you find a preacher serving tables, it is generally because some of us laymen have fallen down on the job.—(3,87)

SMALL GROUPS

. . . I have received a great many blessings from our Share Groups. They have strengthened each of the people who attend, and this has drawn our church closer together. We spend time in prayer, for each other and our pastor. He has grown a great deal due to the prayers of his people. I have learned to love people that I thought I could never love. I am more concerned about others knowing Christ as their Lord and Savior.—Wayne Maddox

. . . It is within this century that small groups have again come of age. Clyde Reid in *Groups Alive—Church Alive* has termed their emergence as literally an explosion. Businessmen are meeting for prayer before work or at lunch; housewives are meeting to share Christ or study the Bible over coffee; others are meeting to seek out the hurting through personal witness and sharing in the mental institutions, ghettos, backyards, schools, and industries of our land—not only here but in every corner of the world.—(2,16)

. . . Groups mature much like the people who compose them. They begin in an infancy of dependence, move through a resistance to any freedom offered them, into adolescent rebellion, a celebration of independence, and finally into mature interdependence composing all the members of the group. Keeping the life cycles in mind helps explain the strange behavior sometimes exhibited by groups.—(2,48)

. . . Tips for Small Groups: (1) Encourage discussion by asking several people to contribute answers to a question. "What do the rest of you think?" or "Is there anything else which could be added?" are ways of encouraging discussion. (2) Be flexible and skip any questions which do not fit into the discussion as it progresses. (3) Deal with irrelevant issues by suggesting again the purpose of your study. Suggest an informal chat about tangential or controversial issues after the regular study is dismissed. (4) Receive all contributions warmly. Never bluntly reject what anyone says, even if you think the answer is incorrect. Instead, ask in a friendly manner, "Where did you find that?" or "Is that actually what it says?" or "What do some of the rest of you think?" Allow the group to handle problems together.

(5) Be sure you don't talk too much as the leader. Redirect those questions which are asked you. A discussion should move in the form of an asterisk, back and forth between members, not in the form of a fan, with the discussion always coming back to the leader. The leader is to act as moderator. As members of a group get to know each other better, the discussion will move more freely, progressing from the fan to the asterisk pattern. (6) Don't be afraid of pauses or long silences. People need time to think. Never, *never* answer your own question—either use an alternate question or move on to another area for discussion. (7) Watch hesitant members for an indication by facial expression or bodily posture that they have something to say, and then give them an encouraging nod or speak their names. (8) Discourage too talkative members from monopolizing the discussion by specifically directing questions to others. If necessary, speak privately to the over-talkative one about the need for discussion rather than lecture in the group, and enlist his aid in encouraging all to partici-pate.—(19,92-93)

. . . Never again will it be just another deacon board, finance committee, or woman's circle. They will be *groups* ready to burst alive under the spirit of Jesus Christ.—(2,21)

. . . The biggest danger of the small group movement is that as individual members begin to get "changed," they sometimes tend to form pious cliques that meet only to mirror their own goodness, and under the guise of study, withdraw from the world rather than seek to be used by God to become his lights in the darkened situations of our communities.—(11,71)

. . . When Christians minister, they must always remember that the "church" is not a building, but rather part of the family of God. Outsiders can be introduced to the "church" without ever setting foot in a sanctuary. The family of God can minister, therefore, in any living room or around any kitchen table. Thousands of Outsiders can be reached from these small-group meetings in homes who would never attend formal religious services.—(19,81)

. . . The old saying that you receive as much as you put into something is true for small groups. The group that requires little will show little and mean little to its members. The disciplines set down must come from within the group and not be imposed on the group from some outside source.

The minimum discipline reproduced below is used by the Yokefellow Groups of Heritage Baptist Church.

(1) The Discipline of Devotion. To read a portion of Scripture and to read and to pray each day, preferably in the morning. (2) The Discipline of Worship. To share at least once each week in church worship. (3) The Discipline of Giving. To share a definite portion of my income in the work of Christ, preferably a tithe. (4) The Discipline of Study. To spend time in the reading of Christian books and articles each week. (5) The Discipline of Ministry. To discover my ministry and to exercise it faithfully in the power of the Spirit. (6) The Discipline of Witness. To share with others, unapologetically, the good news of Christ's ability to save and help. (7) The Discipline of Fellowship. To be involved with specific other Christians in an effort of mutual encouragement.

SPIRIT-FILLED LIFE

. . . The two, *renewal* and the *Spirit-filled life*, are not the same in that the latter tends to be primarily inward and individualistic. Renewal tends to link the individualistic with the corporate dimensions of the faith and to emphasize the necessity of the gathered community, the church. At present the two movements are only beginning to meet, but with immense joint potential. The Spirit-filled life can be the "journey inward" step of renewal and renewal can be the "journey outward" for the deeper life emphasis! Renewal provides a place to go lest the Spirit-filled life become merely a "hot-house" religion, and the Spirit-filled life balances the creative ministry mentality in renewal by stressing those things which "cannot be explained" in terms of human ingenuity and strength, but only "by the Spirit."—(7,24)

. . . F. B. Meyer was a young man who realized that he could not do God's work in his own power. He went to a Keswick meeting. He confessed sin, yielded his will, and prayed. At last he walked down a lonely road, he prayed, "Lord, I've done everything I know and failed. What more must I do to receive your Holy Spirit?" It seemed as though he heard God's voice "F. B., just as by faith you received salvation from the hands of the crucified Christ, so by faith you must receive the infilling of the Holy Spirit from the hands of the resurrected Lord."

At this, Meyer said, "Lord, just as I breathe in this warm air tonight, so by faith I receive your Holy Spirit to control my life."

What happened? F. B. Meyer did not see a bright light. He did not have an ecstatic experience or speak in tongues. The Person of the Holy Spirit flooded his life giving him power to witness to God's Son, Jesus.

. . . There are people who have within them the Spirit of God. A person once asked, "Has Dwight L. Moody a monoply of the Holy Spirit?" "No," someone answered, "but the Holy Spirit has a monopoly of Moody." That great preacher touched the lives of thousands of people. It wasn't because his sermons were better than some other preacher's. It was rather because of the spirit which possessed him. We say of some person, "He has a bad spirit." Of another we say, "He has a good spirit." Of some we say, "He has the Spirit of God."

. . . The reasons some have not experienced the Spirit-filled life are:

(A) A lack of information. Many Christians are ignorant as to what the Bible promises concerning the Spirit-filled life. A student at a Baptist college said, "All this talk of the Holy Spirit is a mystery to me. I've been a member of a Baptist church ever since I was eight years old, and I have never heard anyone preach on the subject of the Spirit-filled life." Fortunately, there is such a reemphasis of the Holy Spirit today that it could almost be claimed the Holy Spirit is no longer the neglected person in the Godhead. Certainly, there is in our generation a welcome renewal of concern about his ministry in the individual, the church, and the world.

(B) Misinformation. Some think that the infilling of the Holy Spirit is for great saints such as Billy Graham, C. L. Culpepper, the apostle Paul, St. Augustine, Ruth Paxson, Bertha Smith, F. B. Meyer, and others. This is not true. The promise and command concerning the infilling of the Spirit are universal. Some feel that unless the infilling of the Spirit is accompanied by the ecstatic or *glossolalia* (speaking in tongues), one has not received the Holy Spirit. This is an unfortunate idea which has caused Christians to shy away from this great spiritual truth. It should be noted that great hosts of people who do not speak in tongues are Spirit-filled. Some feel that God must *send* his Holy Spirit upon us. This is not true. If we are saved, the Holy Spirit is already present in our lives. It is a matter of allowing the Spirit to have control over our lives. The Holy Spirit indwells every believer, but he doesn't fill every believer.

(C) Lack of concern. Many times Christians get busy with good things and forget the most important thing. This is when we quench the Spirit.

(D) Moral hangups. There are many people who are living in open sin. They are disobedient to the Father. There is some moral hangup in their lives, and these people will never know the infilling of the Holy Spirit.

SPIRITUAL DEVELOPMENT

. . . The Christian life throughout is like riding a bicycle, the person must either keep going, or he must fall.—(5,17)

. . . The supreme thing, the paramount thing, the thing God is after above everything else is to produce in this present world men and women who are like the humanity of Jesus Christ. He does not want white-robed saints, or accomplished churchmen, or religious experts; what he wants is that you and I may be grown up, responsible, well adjusted, wholehearted, human beings like Jesus Christ!—(22,117)

. . . It is tragic for a teenager to be experiencing rapid growth in every area of his life except the spiritual. It is sad to see a Christian lawyer who has memorized all of the historic cases of law but who has only a sketchy knowledge of the historic basis of his religion. The young suburbanite who has a better understanding of roses than the spiritual need of her community is a poor witness. For a father to know more about the batting average of his favorite big league team than what is happening spiritually to his son does not make sense. A Christian's spiritual development needs to keep pace with the rest of his life.—(4,32-33)

SPIRITUAL NEUROTICS

. . . There is some danger that at the moment the layman begins to think seriously about his religion, he turns inward, basing nearly everything on his own testimony or the sharing of his testimony with others. Unchecked subjectivism can make a serious layman an ineffectual spiritual neurotic. God never intended for us to find most of our solutions inside ourselves.— (4,10)

TOTAL CONCERN

. . . Total concern is illustrated by an experience of a Mexican-American woman with a church deeply involved in renewal. For months she passed the church building without going in. One day she learned that the church taught persons to read and write. She could do neither and timidly went inside to inquire. Soon she was involved in a literacy program with a Christian woman as a teacher. The study was in the Gospel of John in a simplified translation. After several sessions the woman not only learned to read but took Christ into her life as Lord and Savior. She began to check books out of the church library to improve her reading. At home she read them to her children. One by one they too became Christians. Her husband, noticing the change in family life, inquired about the cause, heard the gospel, and also became a Christian. The woman, embarrassed by her obesity, enrolled in the church's physical fitness program. With pounds trimmed off she needed a new wardrobe. The church's sewing class provided the opportunity for that. With a new life, a new family, a new figure, and a new wardrobe, she reached out to help others. As a worker in a child care program, she now shares the good news with others. Such a story would never have been told if numbers of persons in the church had not discovered their gifts and responded to God's call to minister to the total needs of all persons.—Bill Pinson

VICTORY IN JESUS

. . . A group of college students were at a conference where one young person from each state was to participate in a speakers' tournament. In preparation, one of the young women, who was quite short, checked the microphone and discovered that it was set at least a foot above her head. She tried to adjust it but couldn't. In panic she ran to the person in charge and blurted, "The mike's too high. The mike's too high." The leader, whose sense of humor was well known, calmly replied, "You have ten minutes. Grow!"

I understand the emotion of the young woman. When I am confronted with the world and all its problems and my own sense of inadequacy in meeting the demands of the situation, I have a strong desire to run to my heavenly Father and cry, "The problems are too great. Lower them so I can handle them." Yet I know that this is not the way God helps me. He does not intend to shrink the problems of life to the size of our answers and abilities. But God will nurture and develop his children so that they will be completely adequate for the living of these days. Being a victorious Christian in today's world requires more than we have. But it does not require more than is available.—(4,27-28)

VULNERABILITY

. . . Max Beerbohm once said that all the world is divided into two classes of people: the guests and the hosts. We all know that a guest is someone who is invulnerable, who is waited upon and showered with attention. A host, on the other hand, is one who puts his guests at ease and affirms their worth in a thousand different ways and makes himself vulnerable to them, giving up his privacy and providing food and lodging.

It seems to me that Jesus Christ, who is "the Host" in all of life, is calling those who believe in him to become those who can be vulnerable, put other people at ease, love them, listen to them, and affirm them.— (14,60)

. . . To approach our fellowmen outside the family of faith with an attitude of superiority, power, and extraordinary wisdom will only put them off and diminish the possibility of leading them into a relationship with Christ. But to share our common humanity in an open, vulnerable way is to approach the ideal of servanthood which should be the goal of all Christians in their relationship to the world.—(14,124-125)

WITNESSING

. . . Successful witnessing is sharing Christ in the power of the Holy Spirit and leaving the results to God.

. . . The Holy Spirit is not the one who *helps us* witness; the Holy Spirit *is* the witness. All he needs from you to witness through you is *nothing.* If you will be nothing, he can be everything. Whenever you try to "be something," to that degree you diminish his witness.—(19,51)

. . . We are often reluctant to witness because we do not have any joy in our present relationship. A young student expressed to me what must be the experience of many. He said, "I do not enjoy my job, my wife, my church, or myself. I don't see any sense in spreading my misery." In striking contrast is the testimony of a young executive with whom I was riding to a banquet. I asked how he was doing and he replied, "I've never been happier in my life. For years I've been a believer and active in the church but I'm getting a kick out of it now I never knew before. There was a time when talking me into getting involved in evangelism would have been impossible. But now, when I meet someone who is sharp and exciting, the first thought that comes to my mind is that they ought to get into my church." People who are happy make better witnesses.— (4,129-130)

WORSHIP

. . . True worship, which is always a miracle and a mystery, occurs when the worshiper is confronted by God, hears him, loves him, and feels loved. Praise results. Thus, when John was worshiping, it was only natural that he "heard behind him a great voice." When God speaks and we hear, then worship has occurred. Anything else is but a caricature of worship.— (9,47-48)

. . . Worship is to Christian living what the mainspring is to the watch.— Lawrence R. Axelson

. . . In prayer and worship, one learns that God can use all that one does for his purposes: the frustrations, mistakes, failures—even outright rebelliousness—when they are offered to him. Through prayer and worship all life becomes meaningful and purposeful.—(1,121)

. . . A young man arrived late for church. He asked the usher, "Am I too late for the worship service?" The usher replied, "The worship is over, the service has just begun."

Sources

1. From *The Ministry of the Laity,* by Francis O. Ayres, The Westminster Press. Copyright © MCMLXII, W. L. Jenkins. Used by permission.
2. William Bangham, *The Journey into Small Groups,* (Memphis: The Brotherhood Commission, SBC, 1974).
3. H. C. Brown, Jr., Ed., *Messages for Men,* (Grand Rapids: Zondervan, 1960). Used by permission.
4. Kenneth Chafin, *Help! I'm a Layman,* (Waco, Texas: Word Books, 1966). Used by permission.
5. Theodore H. Epp, *Praying with Authority,* (Lincoln, Nebraska: The Good News Broadcasting Association, 1974). Copyright © 1965 by The Good News Broadcasting Association, Inc. All rights reserved. Used by permission.

6. William R. Grace in article "Proclamation and Witness in the Metropolis," Robert Lee, Ed., *The Church and the Exploding Metropolis,* (Richmond: John Knox Press, 1965).

7. David Haney, *Breakthrough into Renewal,* (Nashville: Broadman Press, 1974).

8. _____, *The Idea of the Laity,* (Grand Rapids: Zondervan, 1973). Used by permission.

9. _____, *The Journey into Life,* (Memphis: The Brotherhood Commission, 1974).

10. _____, *Renew My Church,* (Grand Rapids: Zondervan, 1972). Used by permission.

11. Walden Howard, Ed., *Groups That Work,* (Grand Rapids: Zondervan, 1972). Used by permission.

12. Bruce Larson, *Ask Me to Dance,* (Waco, Texas: Word Books, 1974). Used by permission.

13. _____, *Dare to Live Now!,* (Grand Rapids: Zondervan, 1965). Used by permission.

14. _____, *No Longer Strangers,* (Waco, Texas: Word Books, 1971). Used by permission.

15. John MacArthur, Jr., *The Church the Body of Christ,* (Grand Rapids: Zondervan, 1973). Used by permission.

16. From *The Renewal of the Ministry* by Thomas J. Mullen. Copyright © 1963 by Abingdon Press.

17. Ralph W. Neighbour, Jr., *The Journey into Discipleship,* (Memphis: The Brotherhood Commission, 1974).

18. _____, *This Gift Is Mine,* (Nashville: Broadman Press, 1974).

19. _____, *The Touch of the Spirit,* (Nashville: Broadman Press, 1972).

20. Robert Raines, *New Life in the Church,* (New York: Harper and Row, 1969).

21. Used by permission of Rand-McNally and Company, Chicago, Illinois 60680.

22. From *Body Life* (a G/L Regal Book) G/L Publications, Glendale, CA. 91209, by Ray C. Stedman. © Copyright 1972 by Ray C. Stedman. Used by permission.

23. Elton Trueblood, *Alternative to Futility,* (New York: Harper and Row, 1972).

24. _____, *The New Man for Our Time,* (New York: Harper and Row, 1970).

25. _____, *Your Other Vocation,* (New York: Harper and Row, 1952).

IV TESTIMONIES

In the New Testament, the good news was carried from place to place on the shoulders of personal testimonies. "Come see a man which told me all things that ever I did," urged the woman of Samaria. "Whereas I was blind, now I see," was the straightforward testimony of the blind man. "We have found the Messiah," cried Andrew to Peter. Peter later said, "For we cannot but speak the things which we have seen and heard." The irresistible impulse to share came surging from within.

The personal testimony is one of the secrets of the success of the renewal movement. Turned-on Christians have shared their new-found excitement in Christ. Churchgoers have listened with interest. The Holy Spirit has caused questions to be asked. If that housewife has made Christ Lord; if that lawyer finds time to read the Bible; if that construction worker has a daily prayer life; if that schoolteacher can witness, why can't I? God has used the personal testimony to bring his people back to the basics.

The following testimonies are from people all over the United States. You will notice several common characteristics.

1. No one has a corner on renewal. Laymen, church staff people, and denominational workers are experiencing renewal.

2. Each person testifies to a new excitement in Christ.

3. The lordship of Christ, daily Bible reading, prayer, and witnessing have become a part of life for the renewed persons.

4. Renewal does not bring relief from all problems and heartaches. However, a renewed relationship to God gives added strength in the face of problems.

5. Renewed persons do not feel that they have achieved. They are on a journey with God and in his presence they are happy.

Much benefit will come from reading the testimonies of the working of God in the lives of these renewed Christians.

Sib Sexton; Dentist; Morristown, Tennessee

My wife, Agnes, is a dental hygienist, working one or two days a week in our office, and I am a dentist beginning my eighteenth year in practice.

After much searching, asking questions, and seeking, I crowned Jesus Christ my Lord in November of 1968. I asked him to be the Lord of the 15 percent of me I felt I controlled and to change the 85 percent that I could do nothing with. Previous to this time I had served as a deacon, Training Union leader, choir member, and had participated in other activities of our church. It was not until I crowned Jesus Lord that I began to have peace within.

During the next few years the Lord Jesus became Lord of other areas in my life. In January of 1972, I became involved in a Faith Alive weekend through some friends who encouraged us to attend. At a Saturday morning coffee, the group prayed for me about a problem I had been bothered with for some time. The following Tuesday it occurred to me that the problem was gone and that God would answer prayers. Jesus continued to teach me through tapes, many different people, and experiences. My hunger grew. Agnes continued watching to see if what was happening to me was real. The Lord began to change her as he was changing me. He brought us together and gave us a joyous marriage. Our three children have received the biggest blessing from this because of the love that is now in our home.

Agnes and I had a feeling that we were being prepared for something but didn't know what. A pastor friend of ours arranged a meeting with Reid Hardin at the Holiday Inn in Knoxville, Tennessee, during which he shared the concept of Lay Renewal under the Home Mission Board. After participating in several weekends with Reid and others, I became an associate/coordinator with the Home Mission Board. Agnes and I have been in Lay Renewal Weekends in Tennessee, Georgia, Kentucky, Illinois, and Missouri. We have seen our

Lord use us and others to bring families together, to lead others into a deeper walk with him, to help others to make Jesus their Lord, and to strengthen pastors and churches. One pastor said, "You folks come in right under the defensive radar that a lot of lay people have up." We have seen the lay team members touch people in a way that they can identify. They seem to become more honest and free. As they allow Jesus to take over their life, they begin developing a life-style of sharing, ministering, loving, and walking in the Spirit that they had not known was possible before.

Agnes and I are now involved in discipling some young people in our home after church on Sunday nights. I minister to a coffee house group two or three Saturday nights a month and with the Gideons on Sunday mornings five or six times a year as the Lord leads. We share in our dental practice and have seen some come to know Jesus. As the Lord opens the door, we pray with patients concerning needs shared and find him faithful as we witness answers to prayer. My wife counsels and prays with people on the telephone and at home. Our children are becoming involved as they are growing in the Lord and maturing.

We have not arrived, but we as a family are on a journey with our Lord Jesus Christ that is the most interesting, exciting, and fulfilling way of life we can imagine. There are problems, disappointments, and aggravations from time to time, but our Lord has used them to teach us and enable us to help others. We rejoice at the privilege that our Lord has given us of being a part of what he is doing these days.

Virginia A. Goings; Homemaker; San Antonio, Texas

Lay Renewal Evangelism has changed my life and the life of my family. God loves you and because he loves you, I love you!

James H. Ballard; Pastor; Hialeah, Florida

In 1968 I awoke with a start to realize that I had spent the first ten years of my ministry in a journey through the valley of frustration and desperation. Time spent in introspection shocked me into the reality that during at least one-half of that time God was saying, "I have real fulfillment for you."

The thought was not pleasant as I recalled the fact that at the age of eleven I had accepted Christ and at the age of thirteen I had received the call to be a preacher. My call to the ministry was so definite that I never thought of entering any other field of service. While in college I spent one summer in a pioneer mission effort three thousand miles from home. After seminary I pastored two churches, spent a year on the foreign mission field, and was well into my third pastorate when the frustration with myself and my ministry erupted to the surface.

During the third pastorate I began to feel that if I had to spend the remainder of my pastoral life pumping up leaky programs which had gone beyond their normal amount of mileage, I would never make it. I was strongly tempted to leave the pastorate and to find some other area of service where the median of success would be different and more realistic to me.

Thank God, he did not allow me to go beyond my breaking point. During months of what Georgia Harkness calls "the dark night of the soul," I developed an insatiable desire to read and study. I read every book I could find on the subject of renewal and revival. Eventually it began to dawn upon me that a new day was breaking upon our land. God was speaking to his people across denominational lines. He was leading into exciting, dynamic, vibrant new fields of service in the local church.

This revelation coincided with my first contact with Main Street Baptist Church in Hendersonville, North Carolina. The church possessed a vitality and emphasis on the renewed life that thrilled me. The people at Main Street were talking about God having a very definite mission for their church fellowship. They were interested in ways they could minister to and meet the needs of the community. Their concern was in being the people of God, rather than just increasing in numbers or organization.

The church fellowship had been without a full-time pastor for almost a year, and yet each member of the pulpit committee knew beyond any shadow of doubt that somewhere God had one man he wanted to join with them as their pastor.

As I met with the pulpit committee on a Saturday evening, I sensed God moving in my heart and noted that this group of people struck a chord of spiritual response in me that no one else had ever touched.

The trip back home that evening was made with mixed emotions. Through tear-filled eyes and joy-filled heart I asked God, "What are you trying to dump into my lap?" That week was an exciting one. As I went into the pulpit on Sunday morning, I was aware that a great deal of prayer was being said for me, and I knew that it was going up to God from Hendersonville.

Monday morning began as usual as I went to my study, had my quiet time, and then prepared to study. After my time of devotions, I suddenly found that all of the reading I had been doing for months was coming into focus. I began to write as rapidly as I could, with ideas falling over my pen almost faster than my hand could write them.

At lunch I shared with my wife about my time of renewal and remarked that whether we went to Hendersonville or not, the direction I had received that morning was going to be the approach I would take in my ministry. There was a sense of excitement and anticipation begun that day which has continued with me.

The result of that confrontation with the committee and the breakthrough in my life was that God effected a joining together of a pastor and people in renewal. Being on a common mission in which there were no clergy/laity barriers at Main Street brought forth more honest, meaningful, and relevant confrontation and commitment. An honesty in sharing both the agony and ecstasy of the spiritual pilgrimage brought about a spiritual oneness between pastor and people.

This type of relationship with the members of Main Street Church enabled me to achieve growth in my life that heretofore I had never thought possible. There were times when I led these folk into a deeper understanding of mission, and there were times when they opened my eyes and understanding.

A ministry that is complementing and supplementing is an exciting one. It is also unique, challenging, and exceedingly difficult to program, thank God.

With all of the joy and meaning I was experiencing, I sensed that there was yet a need in my life. I had heard Dr. Stephen Olford from Calvary Baptist Church in New York City speak on several occasions. His message on the victorious Christian life and the Spirit-filled life left me hungry to know more of the abundant life available to God's children. Again I began to study, pray, and search both Scripture and writings of great men of God on the Spirit-filled life.

In February, 1970, I attended a meeting at which Dr. Olford spoke. As he concluded his message, God impressed me with a need to spend time with Dr. Olford and to find that infilling which by then I was seeking. I shared my feelings with Dr. Olford at the conclusion of the service, and he invited me to attend a Christian Life Conference at his church the next month.

However, between that date in February and the conference in March in New York City, something happened. Quietly, but meaningfully, God began to honor my prayer and desire for his infilling of my life. Like a river it flowed silently and deeply. His Word came alive to me in those few weeks as it never had before. I met each day with an inner joy and peace that was unexplainable. Life itself took on a new radiance and dimension. Shortly before I went to New York, I commented to a church member, "I believe I am going for a confirmation of what has already happened to me." It proved to be just that. God had met me in my peculiar need and in my particular now.

For a number of months the Holy Spirit had to clean out garbage which had collected in my life and ministry. His widening of the channels of my life was not always easy, but it was needed. As I experienced spiritual renewal in my life and the joy which came from God's Spirit flowing through me, I became critical of fellow pastors who had not had a renewal experience and who were still searching. God's Holy Spirit dealt with me in this area with two

very definite breakings of my life. One occurred at a renewal conference at Main Street Church led by Ralph Neighbour, Jr., and Findley
Edge. Through their ministry, God convicted me and then broke
me as he revealed my lack of one of the fruits of the Spirit—love.
At a Campus Crusade meeting sometime later I again was shattered
as Dr. Bill Bright asked us to examine our lives as to any sins which
might be there. A few minutes of introspection under the scrutiny
of the Spirit produced five of what the Catholics call the seven
deadly sins. These two experiences of renewal, though not easy, were
needed in my pilgrimage.

These last few years have not been without mistakes on my part
and pruning on God's part. As a pastor involved in a renewing
fellowship, I learned from members as much or more than they
learned from me. It became a joint pilgrimage that strengthened
the bonds of fellowship and love. God began to show us what it
meant to be the Body of Christ . . . to hurt with those who hurt
and to rejoice with those who rejoice. He involved us in ministries
of outreach and concern in working with prisoners, alcoholics, dis-
sident youth, and troubled parents. Our building was used eighteen
hours a day, six days a week.

With the emergence and excitement of renewal happening on
the local level, the church felt called to minister on a larger level.
Renewal conferences were held for three consecutive years 1970-73
as an outreach ministry of Main Street Baptist Church.

From a countyseat town of twenty thousand in Western North
Carolina, God moved me to a metropolitan area of approximately
one and a half million in south Florida. He took me from a young
church with a small membership to a fifty-year-old church of 1750
members. He led me from a vibrant fellowship to one just beginning
in the joy of resurrection. As I look at First Baptist Church in Hialeah,
Florida, and see the evidences of resurrection and renewal, I am
reminded of God's question to Ezekiel, "Can these bones live?"
Ezekiel's answer was, "Lord, you know."

God has brought dynamic life into a church desirous of being
on mission. I see ripples of renewal spreading across the metropolitan

Miami area as members find their mission and ministry in life. As people become anxious for renewal, not only are they experiencing growth in spiritual depth and ministry to one another, but they are being used of God in ever-widening circles. God has given Hialeah First Baptist Church her greatest year yet through the outreach of a growing bus ministry, a school, a Spanish ministry, Bible study groups, and group ministries.

Because of the renewal in my own life, I find the ministry the most exciting place a person can be today. I see myself not only as pastor but also as coach-player and spiritual talent scout. It is thrilling to assist others in discovering their ministries in the body of Christ.

It is good to see old bones live. It is joyous to see God thrusting his people into constantly expanding orbits of ministry and witness. I have come from frustration to fulfillment as a pastor through God's gracious mercy, and in the words of the song, "We've only just begun."

Marie W. McKay; Pastor's wife; Raleigh, North Carolina

As a teenager I read the book *In His Steps* by Charles Sheldon. The question, "What would Jesus do?" became my spiritual helper through those troublesome years of growing toward adulthood.

This same faith led me into marriage and parenthood. Being a mother is a great experience all its own, but being a mother with the help of Jesus Christ is super. No mother has been blessed with any finer sons.

In the fall of 1961 and winter of 1962 I experienced my greatest spiritual growth. We were expecting our fourth child. I was expecting and praying for a girl. After some months had gone by and difficulties arose, my prayer for a girl changed to a prayer for a healthy baby— boy or girl. A little later my prayer turned to something like, "If my baby is not all right, Lord, please let me be all right; I haven't finished all the things I want to do yet."

In another month or two my prayer changed again. This time I simply said, "It doesn't matter what I want, Lord, it's what you want that counts." Those months of turning everything, even my life, over to the Lord, helped me accept the stillbirth of our fourth baby boy. Everything took on a new look to me. Our family had grown closer and our young sons had learned about birth and death in one big lesson. I had a new awareness of Jesus Christ in my life and had experienced the words I remembered from childhood, "Thy will be done."

Another step in my spiritual growth has come about as the result of attending renewal conferences. I like conferences and go whenever I can. In the spring of 1970 I became acquainted for the first time with the term "Lay Renewal." My husband was employed at the time by the Home Mission Board and had been asked to share in a Layman's Landing Conference at the Florida Baptist Assembly. It was April, and going to Florida was a delight. Little did I realize all the happenings and events that would follow that conference.

After my initiation into renewal, I realized I was not sharing with others my joy in Christ. I had a strong faith, a deep joy in knowing I was in Christ, but because I was married to a minister I thought he could do the sharing for both of us. I have come to realize I am responsible for making my life count. No one, not even a minister husband, could do that for me. One of the ways I think most important is simply living my Christian faith.

That is where the *present* comes in. Jesus helps me do some things I know I should, but find difficult to do alone. He also helps me say "no" to things I might like to do, but are not Christian.

This past weekend, I participated as a team leader in a Renewal II weekend in my own church. I am delighted to see others search and find the service gifts God has given them.

As for the future—I have many things planned for the second half of my earthly life. I know Jesus will guide me each step of the way. That's not the end.

Patience Strong wrote a poem that contains this line, "This life is just a sweet, faint hint of life that is to be."

I intend to find out what that other life is all about.

James Smith; Construction worker; Deer Park, Texas

On Saturday morning at 9:30 I was sitting comfortably in my living room chair. I was in for the surprise of my life. My wife said, "Honey, don't you think you had better get ready for the coffee?" I replied, "I have plenty of time since it is at 10:00 this evening." "Oh, no," she said, "it's 10:00 this morning! The folks will be here in about ten to fifteen minutes."

I had no place to go so I slipped on some better clothes and tried to play a good host. As the group shared what Jesus Christ meant to them, I could see that I had a peculiar group of people in my home. When it came my time to share, I stated the truth. I knew I was a Christian but was out of fellowship with the Lord. For some reason I did not have a desire to get back in church and Christian service.

The meeting in my home was over shortly. I cannot tell you how but at the noon luncheon during the Renewal Weekend, I found myself listening to various laymen give their testimonies. One layman in giving his testimony, did not talk about himself. Instead, he talked about me. He began telling what a fine Christian he thought I was. He recalled that several years before I had refused to work on a brewery at a time when construction work was slow. What he did not know was that I was seeking praise not for the glory of God but for the glory of myself. He also did not know that just the day before I had been drinking the product of the brewers art. How I wished he would shut up and sit down. Finally, he did.

The lay coordinator called upon someone to close the meeting in prayer. Before prayer could be offered, another person said, "Wait a minute. James Smith must have such a great testimony. Why don't we let him speak a few words?"

That was when God gave James Smith a whipping. I was brought to realize in just a few seconds that I did not have a witness or testimony for my Lord Jesus Christ. In a very short time God brought me out of the hogpen of sin and put me back in the fold of the church and in service for him.

At last I have found the joy I was seeking in the ways of the world where it is impossible to find. My turn-around that began in a Lay Renewal Weekend has continued in a renewal that is daily.

Wanda Barker; Nurse; Annapolis, Maryland

My journey into renewal has no end; but it does have a very definite beginning. I had been a Sunday School teacher for many years, had taken all the study courses, attended conferences at Ridgecrest, and done many things that good Christians are supposed to do. Although the operating of God in my life was significant, I was caught up in the "syndrome of doing." I had an almost legalistic approach to winning God's favor. Eight years ago we had a pastor who did not please me. He was not fulfilling my needs, so I became very critical of him. When he resigned, I had great expectations that now everything would be just fine.

However, it did not happen that way. We could not get a new pastor for our church for almost a year. As a matter of fact, two preachers who did not even have a church turned us down. They had no place to go, yet they turned us down! I began to realize that the problem was with the church, not with the pastor. This evaluation eventually forced me to look into myself. In choir one Sunday morning I prayed that if God would send us a pastor—his choice—I would not criticize him. I would uphold him and give him my total support no matter what.

When David Haney, our new pastor, arrived two or three months later, one of the first things he did was to teach the book of Acts on Sunday evenings. He emphasized the Holy Spirit in the individual life and the importance of the ministry of the laity. A few months later, a choice servant of God presented a series of sermons on the deeper life. Several church members met in homes after each sermon. The dialogues were so exciting that I asked our pastor if he would meet with us regularly for more. We began meeting one Saturday night a month, and our Yokefellows group was born (Matt. 11:29-30).

About this time I had also been asked to start and teach a young couples' class. Bill and Nancy were the first couple to come and together we visited others. We began to grow in numbers, depth, and willingness to share our faith with others. As new couples came to the church services, I invited them to dinner on the Saturday evening that the Yokefellows met. The constant affirmation from the Sunday School class, the Yokefellows group, and the sermons on commitment and ministry became an integral part of my journey.

The journey with Christ had another phase for me—that of the journey into learning. My son had gone to college to study for the ministry, and he kept coming home with new ideas and theories. Many of them were totally foreign to my doctrines. To keep the lines of communication open with him, I began reading.

Things were not as smooth as they might seem. My son decided not to go into the ministry, and rejected what seemed like all of my values in his search for his own identity. This hurt very deeply. During this time of struggling with my pain, I received a call from a close friend who said she felt the Lord was leading her to ask my husband and me to take a young lady into our home who had many problems including deep depression. I replied, "The Holy Spirit has not said a thing to me about it yet." However, Kathy did arrive. Her looks said, "hippy" and I felt a deep revulsion against that type. She had a prejudice against middle class, suburban, white, Anglo-Saxon Protestants. However, when she allowed me to see beneath her facade, I found a beautiful person, and I needed that. It pointed out the fallacies of my own prejudices.

At first she had no belief in God at all. But after many late-night talks and much reading of some of my books, she had a beautiful conversion experience. One of the wonderful parts of her stay in our home was the help she gave me in understanding the struggles my son was having in finding himself. God seems to have a way of working on me at the same time he is using me.

The following year Ralph Neighbour came to our church explaining his concept of TOUCH ministries used at the West Memorial Baptist Church in Houston, Texas. I had felt a nagging restlessness about my occupation as a legal secretary for some time. As I listened to Ralph Neighbour, I started thinking about and looking for my ministry. Kathy worked at a state mental hospital not far from Annapolis. Thinking it might help me in dealing with young couples in my Sunday School class, she told me about a training program in family therapy offered to nonprofessionals. I took it. Only a few weeks into this training, my employer asked me one morning if I was happy in my job. I replied no, and after nine years as his employee, he asked me to find something else. While this was a terrible blow to my ego, I was able to see God's hand in it. On my own I might never have had the courage to change jobs at the age of forty-nine. I am now working at the state mental hospital.

One important thing I have learned about reaching others is to be sensitive to the Holy Spirit and to wait for a person to give a clue. This became very evident during my first month at the hospital when a young lady waiting to see the psychologist sat by my desk. She was wanted by the FBI for counterfeiting. She was a prostitute. She had attempted suicide. All in all, her life was a mess. In our conversation I asked her if she knew how long her sentence might be.

She: I hope and pray not too long.

Me: Oh, do you believe in prayer?

She: I used to, but not any more.

Me: What happened to make you disbelieve?

She: I can't believe in a just God that would let my father die.

Me: We all die. Is it "that he died" or "when he died" that bothers you?

She: When he died, I guess.

Me: If you were God, when would you have let him die?

Seeing how impossible it was to make that decision, she started to cry. We then could talk about how much God loved her. After two or three days of talks, she had a beautiful experience with Christ. After her discharge from the hospital she wrote glowing letters of answered prayer. When I saw her again two years later, it was hard to believe she was the same person. Her whole appearance had changed.

In 1972 a new superior arrived at the hospital. He limited my working with patients. From previous experience, restlessness seemed to be a way of God's speaking to me so I asked, "Lord, where do you want me to go from here?" As I turned to him, a new opportunity opened whereby I could change job classifications at the conclusion of an educational program.

Entering college at my age and associating with young people right out of high school was both intimidating and challenging. I had intended to study and mark time until I finished but God is at work in colleges, too. I was asked by the professor one day in class why I always seemed so happy and serene. She could have asked any question out of the textbook and not frightened me as much. I was aware immediately that I was being put to the test but the Holy Spirit allowed me courage to give Christ the credit. From that experience, Diane came into my life (another atheist). As I write this, eighteen months later, she has just returned from her first Lay Renewal Weekend where she influenced many people as she shared her search for Christ, and the struggles she is still having surrounded by a family that does not believe.

I have discovered that God works renewal into every area of life, not just the "spiritual." As the journey has deepened, I am more and more aware of the need for a closer relationship in my marriage. God has blessed me with a wonderful Christian husband who is very supportive of me in my efforts to become what God wants me to be. Also, my daughter, who has always shown me acceptance even when I was not very acceptable, I owe so much. And now my son, with his own emerging identity is a much more beautiful person than if he had remained in my image for him.

Nothing that I have said can convey the emotional aspects of my renewal journey. I have had some mountaintop experiences that seemed like total and perfect communion with God. Sometimes I think that heaven must be like that continually. But being human, and imperfect, and sinful, and, sometimes, out of touch with God, I do not always live on that plane. Renewal means commitment; no matter what, I belong to God. Even when I am doubtful or down, I am his.

There have been wonderful things happening in the past eight years on the journey and there have been many struggles that have eventually strengthened me. Where am I now?—anticipating with some anxiety, to be honest, but also much excitement where that journey into the future will take me.

William H. Bolick; Pastor; Laredo, Texas

Renewal for me is a *process*. If it is thought of as an "end"—it is the *beginning end.*

James E. Watson; Manager, automobile company; Brown Deer, Wisconsin

At age nine I was aware of my sin and as so many preachers and evangelists had said there in our church in St. Louis, I was bound for hell. I wanted to go to heaven. It was Easter Sunday, my twin sister was going forward, so I went along. I really did believe that by going forward to be saved, something would happen that would not only bring forgiveness and remove the guilt for my past sins but would also bring about a change that would help keep me out of future sin. When the pastor shook my hand, asked the questions and presented me to the church on my profession of faith, I did not feel any differently. I decided that it would somehow happen later when I was to be baptized. As the pastor performed the symbolic burial and I left the baptismal pool, I realized that the only change which had taken place was that I had entered as a dry sinner and emerged as a wet one. There had been no change at all.

Thus began my "Christian life." It became more like a "spiritual roller coaster." The Watsons were good Baptists. We were at church no matter what was going on. For revivals, study courses, Training Union, prayer meetings, you name it, we were there. There were the dedications and rededications, the commitments and recommitments, but for Jimmie, there was also the ever increasing involvement in sin. For thirteen years I lived a double life. By thought, action, example, and speech, I had made my "Declaration of Independence" from God. Worldliness in form of bad habits, vulgar and profane speech, lying and dishonesty had culminated in a ruined marriage, guilt, frustration, and failure on every hand. I was convinced that sin promises way more than it can deliver and that sinning only degrades, defiles, defeats, and destroys. Recently my wife and four daughters and I were making a trip back to Missouri. We were in the camper going through Iowa. It was a long, flat, bleak stretch of the highway. We saw a hitchhiker up ahead, sitting on the ground with his back against a sign post. He was holding a placard which we were able to read as we passed. It said, "ANYWHERE BUT HERE." I believe the hopelessness expressed by the hitchhiker typifies the wretchedness I felt as a twenty-two-year-old there in St. Louis.

It was during that year that God sent Billy Graham to St. Louis for his first evangelistic crusade in that city. Man, I was ready. I went because I knew that my only hope had to be in making peace with God. Conviction came as Billy Graham talked about the *real* Christian life. Forcefully he impressed me with the fact that Christianity is not "churchanity," external ritualism or an organization to respect. It is a dynamic, exciting, daily experience. A person to accept, a new life to live. I went back a second and a third time. It was on a Thursday night that I went forward, publicly accepting Christ as Lord of all. It was a serious surrender to God's will for all of life. The awareness that God loved *me* personally, that he, through his Spirit would help me to live, one day at a time, for him. Peace at last.

Many of the sins of my life were wiped out immediately. The profanity, lying, immorality, dishonesty, the guilt, and frustrations were cleansed almost instantly. Smoking which had been such a barrier to separate me from victorious Christians and family seemed to be Satan's key to my life. As I left Kiel Auditorium that night, I knew that the two mountains I would have to climb were completing my neglected education and overcoming cigarettes. At age thirty-three I finally received my bachelor's degree. It was five years later that victory came over smoking. As a young Christian of twenty-two and twenty-three years of age, I was praying for power and opportunity which God could not grant until fifteen years later when this barrier to spiritual blessing was finally destroyed.

Many opportunities opened to me as a young man: teaching an adult men's Bible class, summer missions in Washington state, BSU leadership, supply preaching, part-time music director, educational director, and part-time pastor. My business life was also interesting and rewarding. Several years ago while serving as part-time youth director in a large church in the Kansas City area, I was having considerable difficulty finding workers for the youth Sunday School classes and Royal Ambassadors. Many of the folks were content to let the paid help carry the load. We had a fine older deacon who would come by often to talk. As the conversation turned to the great need for workers and the hesitance of most folks to get involved, Floyd, with tears in his eyes would say that what was needed was "new blood." I thought that he was talking about an influx of new people but I came to find out that the "new blood" which was needed was something else.

Poor attendance at past revivals had convinced the church fathers that revivals just were not worth the expense and bother. We all felt that the church needed what a good revival could do for it. One of the deacons had heard about revival coming to a church through a Lay Renewal Weekend. He succeeded in arranging a meeting with a Texas layman who was a coordinator, and he came to meet with the church staff and the deacons. The date was set for our weekend, and we went to work making preparations. Everywhere you would look there were signs, "Expect a miracle" and "Pray for a miracle." I did pray, but I did not see how God could really solve our problems through a bunch of laymen during a forty-two-hour weekend program. Then, all of a sudden, they arrived. They had come more than five hundred miles, at their own expense, by bus, car, and plane. There were nearly one hundred of them. They were everywhere; happy, smiling, telling everyone, "God loves you and I love you" and meaning it. They were just ordinary folk but they, like all the other witnesses I have come to know, were excited about Jesus. The only conversation topic which interested them was about God's love, his Son, his leadership and purpose for life. It was all so simple: sharing, praying, singing, self-examination, concern, and most of all, love. The object of it all was to present total commitment to Christ as the way, the only Christian way to live. During the invitation on Sunday morning when scores of people came down and at the evaluation service on Sunday night, it was obvious that miraculous things had taken place in the lives of most of our people. The "new blood" of Christ had cleansed away much of the old indifference, worldliness, and aimlessness which had produced fruitlessness in many lives. People got excited about things of the spirit and went to work for the Lord. The problem of finding workers was completely resolved.

There were many prayer and share groups which were formed in homes as a result of the renewal. They became powerful centers for spiritual power and victory. The youth share group met for several years in our home. In sharing how they handled temptations and problems, these young people were able to uphold one another. Their excitement about Jesus, their willing witness, the singing, and sharing became a significant force for good in the lives of many young people.

I became convinced that God had carefully prepared me for a task which was not, as yet, being accomplished. I had a good job as senior process engineer at the Ford Motor Co. assembly plant in Kansas City. Long overtime hours and increased responsibility had made it impossible for me to devote the necessary time to the youth program at church, and I had felt compelled to resign. I prayed that if God had a job for me elsewhere that he would open the doors and lead me to move. A short time later I received a call from an executive search company with an offer from my present employer but at the Toledo Jeep Plant. I requested prayer at the youth prayer and share group and went for the interview. All went well and I felt sure that an offer would come. Finally, I received word that my management experience was inadequate and that they would continue their search. I accepted this as God's answer, as a closed door, as God indicating that I was to stay where I was. I came to find out that the young people had prayed that I would stay in Missouri. A few months later I received another call, same company, same job, different location so I prayed, "Father, if you want me here in Missouri, I'll stay a hundred years. If you want me to go to Milwaukee, open the doors." I was hired.

As a summer missionary in the Pacific northwest, I had been thrilled by the challenge of pioneer missions. Now I am living in pioneer territory for Southern Baptists. The need for committed, enthusiastic laymen in this area is staggering. The Lord has opened more avenues for service during our first fifteen months here than he has ever before. Because of my involvement in Lay Renewal as a youth coordinator for over thirty Lay Renewal Weekends, I have been elected as Director of Baptist Men for Lakeland Baptist Association.

In addition to assisting many of our pastors with lay pulpit supply, I have had the opportunity to assist three of our sixteen churches with preparations for Lay Renewal. As the excitement builds, it is not difficult to foresee that God is preparing to use this wonderful experience of renewal to give our pioneer efforts the needed spark to become a vital force in meeting the spiritual needs of this area. I thank God that he has prepared me and called me to have a part in this Spirit-filled movement.

Barbara Perkins; Pastor's wife; Oklahoma City, Oklahoma

We had our Lay Renewal Weekend and talk about showers of blessing! I've never seen anything like it in all my life. People started tithing and having family worship and witnessing and confessing sins and fasting. One could hardly find a place near the altar steps to kneel and pray. A hardened man found the Lord about 1:30 A.M. Sunday at the altar. As for the Sunday services, our people would hardly leave at 1:00 P.M. for lunch! (Western Hills is noted for its people liking their Sunday lunch on time!) The Sunday night service ran four hours. The Western Hills lay people took over the service with their testimonies and prayer requests and eagerness to sing, even spontaneous duets! I tell you, if it gets any better around here, I won't be able to stand it! They don't need a preacher any more—they just need someone to direct traffic around the altar!

Vernon Brinkley; Airline pilot; Hico, Texas

My life had always been a series of goals which did two things. They occupied my mind and absorbed my energy. They also served to give me a purpose in life and to fill the God-shaped vacuum in me. At the age of thirty-three, I'd accomplished all my goals from high school football, to college degree, to a set of Air Force wings, to a position as an airline pilot. I was economically and socially secure. All of a sudden without any goals left, I felt a weakness and emptiness. No matter how hard I tried, I could not escape. Through my wife's salvation and the change in her, I began to read the Bible in secret. I read through Matthew and half-way through Mark when I fell in love with the person of Jesus Christ and on April 4, 1972, I publicly gave my life to Christ.

The next six months I spent in the process of growth by Bible study and prayer and fully enjoying my newfound, exciting life. After about six months, I felt a new strange feeling that there was something I was supposed to be doing and wasn't and I didn't know what or where. I only felt it was something that was to be done as a family. I was led to call the man that was my pastor when I accepted the Lord and discuss my feelings with him. I felt like I'd be willing to put on sackcloth and ashes and go to the streets of Dallas if the Lord would just let me know what I was to do. My pastor suggested that perhaps I should consider working in the area of renewal. I agreed to try, and it was arranged for my wife and I to be invited to my first Renewal Weekend.

For the first time in my short experience as a Christian, I saw a new joy and expression of God's love that I'd not seen before. I knew I'd found where God wanted me. I felt that if I could spend the rest of my life as a team member, I would be happy, but the Lord had other ideas. I attended a WIN School and a few weeks later a second phase of the Lay Renewal Weekend. This weekend was geared to the discovery of God's will and purpose in our lives. On Sunday morning, I felt that I was to become a coordinator in

Lay Renewal. The small group of which I was a part commissioned me into this area of service. About a minute after this took place, the coordinator came up to me and asked me to lead the worship service. This was something I had never done and had no training in at all. However, I'd just agreed to serve the Lord as a coordinator and the Lord was about to show me that if I gave myself, he would give me the ability. At the morning worship I knew that I was at home as a coordinator and again felt a special closeness to the Lord. I also felt I had the answer for modern Christianity. I couldn't understand why everyone else did not feel the way I did. I wanted to go everywhere I could to explain the movement and defend it.

I learned through this experience a special understanding and compassion for the troubles and fears of pastors in relation to their flocks and individual laymen, which is to this day a burden I still carry. In spite of the few that rejected the movement, there were many more that accepted and were blessed by it. This gave me the assurance that God had truly blessed the movement and that it was going along just as he had planned.

I thought that would be the end of my journey. Now I would settle down to an occasional Renewal Weekend and enjoy life. I was in for a shock. Our state needed someone to work in renewal full time. The Executive Director of Texas Baptist Men said, "Vernon, I think the Lord wants you to take a six months leave of absence and help us coordinate Renewal Weekends." Immediately I thought of the pay cut and other obvious reasons for rejecting the offer. Through prayer it became obvious that this was God's will for my life. "Okay," I said, "I'll do the work and let you do the worrying." The Lord truly blessed us and the Lay Renewal Weekend movement. We have grown from one to two weekends a month to as many as twenty and from ten coordinators to nearly sixty. We have, at the invitation of the Foreign Mission Board, held weekends in the Bahamas and Madrid, Spain.

The renewal movement has been the vehicle that the Lord has given me to enjoy my salvation. It is my ministry. I rejoice that the Lord has called me at an early age from being a total unbeliever to having a position in God's army.

L. D. Galyean; Communication engineer; Houston, Texas

I was raised in a Christian home and until I left to go to college, I never knew anything other than a church-oriented family. After leaving home and coming in contact with the outer world, I drifted in and out of fellowship with Christ.

I went through World War II and was saved many times from death, all the time knowing that it was through the grace of God and because he had something for me to do. All the while I kept running from the Lord and telling myself that there was nothing I could do to serve his purpose. I was miserable in going to church, so I was a Sunday morning Christian when I felt like going.

After almost ruining my life and almost turning my wife and children away from me, I realized that something had to change. I thought I had recommitted my life anew to Christ, and began attending church in earnest. I became a teacher of a men's Bible Class, president of the Brotherhood and chairman of the Stewardship Committee. Still, I was unhappy in this service. Then came Lay Renewal, and I found what total commitment really meant. That weekend, I truly surrendered my will to him for whatever he wanted me to do. I was reluctant because I had always been shy and backward around crowds. The Lord took all this away and indicated that he wanted me to be a coordinator for Lay Renewal Weekends. I can truthfully say that these past two years have been the happiest of my lifetime. My family's life has been touched in a way that words cannot describe.

Through these Renewal Weekends, we have been able to be instruments of Jesus to touch the lives of people and churches that could never be done in any other way. All of this is because we have been able for the first time in our lives as a family, to pray and ask Christ to just let us get ourselves out of the way and let him work his will through us, all the while realizing that it is his work and none of ours.

During a Renewal Weekend in a small church we discovered that the pastor's twenty-year-old wife came from a broken home and had never had any parental love. At the altar service on Saturday night my wife and I adopted her as our daughter. This has touched two families in a way in which the results will never be known. We can give her the parental love she has never had. She can fill the place of a daughter which we never had. All through the grace and love of our Jesus Christ who loves us so.

Martha Lipford; Homemaker; Palm Springs, California

About four years ago I began to look at my life. I saw a person that I really didn't like. I had held, at one time or another, every office in the church and served on almost every committee. Of course, I had never been a deacon or a pastor, but almost everything. However, I would find myself saying, "Am I just playing church or is this for real?" I would look back and see no results from the things I had been doing and no souls added to God's kingdom. Yet everything seemed so important at the time.

In 1972 we went to Glorieta for Home Missions Week. My husband, John, attended a conference on Lay Renewal. I chose to go to another conference. After two days I joined John for the rest of the week. The meaning of the renewal conference didn't get through to me, but John came away very excited. On the rest of our trip all my husband could talk about was Lay Renewal. I wasn't impressed at all. I viewed it as more duties and responsibilities. I've never been one to talk back or refuse my husband what he says is best. I went along, but not in a pleasant way. This caused problems in our home.

The following summer we went back to Glorieta and again attended the conference on Lay Renewal. During this time I had decided that Reid Hardin, director of Lay Renewal with the Home Mission Board, was the cause of all my problems. I had built up a hatred for him over the past year. I had nothing good to say about *him* or *his* program. He asked us to go to Ridgecrest that same month. During this time the Lord kept telling me that the problem was me. In Ridgecrest we talked much about loving each other. It was at this point that I saw that Satan had been using

Reid Hardin to keep my eyes off of what God wanted for my life. I asked the Lord to forgive me. Then the Lord showed me that I should go to Reid and ask forgiveness. It took a lot of doing on my part to admit I had been wrong and ask forgiveness from a man I hardly knew. God was with me.

I can see now that the Lord had to change many of my attitudes and feelings for him, the church, my life, my home, and my family before he could really use me effectively. I had never really shared myself with people other than my own and the church family. I was always too busy in the church to see outside the four walls of the building. In the first Renewal Weekend we were instructed to say, "God loves you and I love you." I began to realize that I wasn't letting Jesus love people through me. I can't begin to put in writing all the struggles I've had the last three years. However, I have learned that when I seek his will for my life, he will put me where he wants me and give me the strength to do his will.

I praise God for Lay Renewal and how it has changed my life.

Fred and Gloria Roach, Executive Vice-President, Home Builder and Homemaker; Miami, Florida

About five years ago we learned our church was to have a Lay Renewal Weekend. We weren't exactly sure just what this would prove to be but we were curious—and quite truthfully we had a need for renewal in our lives. Things were not just right between us and the Lord. We weren't experiencing any joy. In fact there was a coldness, almost a hardness, in our relationship with him and other Christians much of the time. Everything seemed like such a routine. We were in our places each Sunday and Wednesday. We enjoyed the places of church responsibility we had, but there was something missing!

On the Friday night of the Renewal as we gathered together in our Fellowship Hall, a group of strangers came into our midst. They were dressed ordinarily enough, but right away we noticed something special about them. They seemed to have a certain glow on their faces! They smiled and talked to us. They were really interested in us. They even listened to us!

Later in the evening they shared what God had done and was doing in their lives. They talked of the freedom they had found in Christ, the need for relying on the power of his Spirit (and not ourselves), and how we commit our lives *daily* to Christ. Some shared how they had learned that emotions are tricky. They suggested that we cannot depend upon our feelings, but upon the truth of the Word of God. They related very personal experiences of how God was changing them and how prayer and Bible reading had taken on new meaning.

As we listened, our hearts were responding, "Yes, Lord, that's what we want—more of you, less of self."

As we broke into sharing groups that night and the following, we examined our lives even further. We learned the wonderful joy that comes from praising God and bearing testimony of him. It was great to be in a group of fellow church members where the topic of conversation was Jesus Christ!

Because we had a need and because we were willing, Jesus became *real* in our lives once again. Praise God! It's getting better all the time!

La Rue Hagan Wyatt; Homemaker; Corsicana, Texas

Before Lay Renewal came to my church, I had never given a personal testimony. I had always been ashamed of mine because it wasn't very pretty. I knew if I gave a testimony, I would have to be honest. I was afraid if I told the truth about myself, no one would love me.

I've always been amazed at the fact that God could have wanted me in the first place. I was raised in a broken home where the only time I ever heard God's name mentioned was when it was taken in vain. My mother was an alcoholic and finally committed suicide. In time God provided me with a Christian husband who led me to Christ through his deep devotion to the Lord.

Because of my background, I built a wall around myself so no one could hurt me. The wall was so thick that nothing but fear could penetrate it. I figured if I didn't show my feelings to anyone, then it wouldn't matter if I was loved in return or not. For many years I had let the scars of my past cheat me out of God's blessings and the love of my church.

I was bitter inside and resentful towards Christians in general. They had never helped my mother and I felt they wouldn't help me either. What a wall! The only thing it did was keep me bottled up inside. I was like acid inside and so unhappy as a Christian.

God knew this. He also knew that my mother-in-law was the most important woman in my life. She had literally taken the place of my mother. One week before our Lay Renewal, my mother-in-law did not report for work. I had to break into her kitchen to get to her. This petrified me because it had only been a few years since my mother was found dead in her bed. The only thing I could think of was, "Oh, no, not again. Don't let me go in there and find her dead, too."

She lay in a coma suffering from spinal meningitis for five days. Her doctor told me that she couldn't possibily live because her vital life signs were failing. He also said that there was a greater physician than himself, and it was up to him now. All this time, day and night, my church was with me. I never knew how much they loved me. Maybe I should say I never realized it before because I never gave them the chance to show me.

I was so helpless and bewildered at the hospital. I loved her so much, and I needed a mother so badly. I wanted to tell her how much she had meant to me. That week was the first time I had ever truly thought of Christians as really being my brothers and sisters in Christ.

In my grief that week I poured out my heart to Christian friends. They cried with me, prayed with me and for me. Most important of all, they verbally told me how much they loved and cared for me. That did it! That wall around me crumbled into a million pieces, and I was at last willing to trust others to love and accept me as I was. I wasn't alone any more. Love conquered my fears and my past didn't matter. I now know that not only does God love me,

but his people love me, too. I no longer have to worry about the
past and I am confident about the future.

God is so good; he's so good to me.

LaVerne Hale; Farmer's wife; Mullin, Texas

For a long time my spiritual life stayed on the level of Luke
2:52, "And Jesus increased in wisdom and stature, and in favour
with God and man." Then I was offended in my church. I had taught
four- and five-year-olds for twenty-five years then someone had
the nerve to tell me that I was not doing what I should. While
I carried my grudge around on my sleeve, many strifes came into
my life. One day I read in 1 Peter 4:12-19 that if I suffer as a
Christian I have become more like Christ. This thrilled me to think
that I had suffered like Jesus did, and I was more like him. I still
carried the grudge. On another occasion I was repeating the Lord's
Prayer and came to the part that said, "Forgive us our debts, as
we forgive our debtors." I realized that I had to forgive others before
Jesus could forgive me.

I found this was easy to do for everyone except my husband. Then
a group of people came to our church for a Lay Renewal Weekend.
One of the ladies said, "Ladies, we must be submissive to our hus-
bands." She even repeated the Scripture passage in Ephesians. This
did something to me. I realized I had to get the sin of pride and
rebelliousness out of my life. Although it was difficult, and still is,
I have learned the truth of submission.

After a year of Lay Renewals, I have grown more as a Christian
than all the other years of my Christian life. I have learned that
God's grace is sufficient for me, that he can guard me from the
devil. I would like to praise God that he can take a weak Christian
like me and intercede for me in prayer as it says in Romans 8:26,
and then tell me that "we are more than conquerors through him
that loved us" (Rom. 8:37). There is no way anyone can stop me
from being a victorious Christian after reading verse 39, "Nor height,
nor depth, nor any other creature, shall be able to separate us from
the love of God, which is in Christ Jesus our Lord."

Oran Henderson; Electronics technician; Gatesville, Texas

I love to work in the church for Jesus, whereas before Lay Renewal it was a huge task to do anything in the church! How thankful I am that Lay Renewal came my way before the Lord spewed me out of his mouth for I was certainly, *at best,* lukewarm! Of course, the devil didn't bother me much before Lay Renewal. (I was doing just what he wanted me to—nothing.) He appears very often now, but Jesus knows how to handle him!

My goal from now on is total commitment of my life to Christ, and I do my best to commit as much of myself as I can to as much of God as I understand each day.

Leonard Hinton, Jr.; Research consultant; Atlanta, Georgia

"And this is the secret: *that Christ in your hearts is your only hope of glory*" (Col. 1:27, TLB). Yes, this is my hope of glory—the fact that Jesus Christ is living in my heart. I came to know him at an early age, largely because of the influence of my Christian family. While I was pursuing an engineering career, God called me into a full-time Christian vocation of research with the Sunday School Board and later with the Home Mission Board. After many years of trying to live an active Christian life I came to have a deep hunger for a closer fellowship with the Lord. In 1969 God led me into a meaningful renewal experience involving confession of sins, yielding of self and receiving a fulness of his love and peace. Since then, even through problems, there has been a growing realization of the power and presence of Jesus Christ in my life.

As I have sought to keep my commitment to Christ current by being available to him day by day, the Lord has opened many doors. A most significant opportunity occurred in October of 1972 when I, along with others, committed myself to a renewal journey with a somewhat open agenda as to what God might do. Colossians 1:29 expresses my personal sense of mission as a Renewal Associate: "This is my work, and I can do it only because Christ's mighty energy is at work within me" (TLB).

One of my greatest joys in renewal came during a second renewal weekend as I saw the great growth that had occurred in so many people between the first weekend and the second. During the second weekend almost all of the team members were from the local church. What a wonderful team it was, as we shared and prayed together and felt God working and moving in our lives! During the weekend I was given the opportunity of teaching the learning sessions and coming to feel the very heartbeat of the church.

Let me share briefly a part of the story of one very precious couple to illustrate what had been happening in the church. As you know, one of the special blessings of a renewal weekend is in knowing the hospitality and fellowship of staying in the home of some of the church people. It was our privilege this time to be the guests of Newton and Julia Manly and to have times of personal sharing with them. Oh, how evident was God's work in their lives and their growth in him since the first weekend. During the first weekend Newton was in my Saturday night small group session. He requested prayer and through the prayer of several of his friends, God touched his life in a very real and meaningful way. I learned later that during the coffee sharing period that same day, Julia, his wife, was also definitely touched by the Lord. That Saturday night of the first weekend this couple returned home after the session at church and prayed together on their knees in a new and exciting experience of prayer.

Since that time, Newton and Julia have been open and willing to allow God to continue to do his work in their lives. They are now having a prayer and sharing group in their home each week. They are also ministering to many married and single young people in the church. The fruit of their service was in evidence as Newton and Julia were affirmed many times during the second weekend by people whose lives God has touched through them. When I see what God can do in lives yielded to him, I just want to say, "Praise the Lord."

Nell Shotwell; Newspaper columnist; McGregor, Texas
My first impression of Lay Renewal came when a friend from

another denomination told us of something unusual happening in their church and invited us to the Sunday night service. There we heard testimonies from the young and old telling of how they were resolved to live more closely to the Lord. We did not know what had gone before, but we were impressed by the sincerity of those we heard.

A little over a year later, my daughter and I had moved to another town because of the death of my husband and in order to be near some of our family. After a few months, I had joined First Baptist Church of McGregor, Texas, and later was teaching a Sunday School class. Because of what I had heard in the other church, I was ready to assist in preparation for and expected something interesting to happen during our Lay Renewal weekend. However, I did not expect it to have a great impact on my life, because I was fairly regular in church attendance, read my Bible almost daily, and asked God for guidance in decisions that had to be made. I was aware of God's love and guidance since the death of my husband and a very beloved sister-in-law, but often felt sorry for myself and probably showed it.

It was a pleasure to have two young ladies stay with us for the Lay Renewal. My daughter was a college student at Baylor University and dedicated to the Lord, studying church music. The testimonies of the team members and the association with Bob and Jean Dixon, our coordinators, were rewarding. At the small group sharing sessions, I began to see that my spiritual life was shallow, and that I was not giving myself wholly to the Lord. As the question, "Are you seeking the total will of God in your life?" was put to us, I began to ask myself how I could be used to fulfill God's mission for my life.

At the Sunday night service after the visiting laymen had gone home, I told the church that I felt the Lord had a work for me to do during the remainder of my life. I did not know yet what it would be, but I was determined to seek his will. I realize now that I had been led in many ways to that point in my life.

The first thing I did was to volunteer to go as a witness on a Lay Renewal weekend to another church. I was invited and took part in several and each was a blessing to me. I am not sure how much I was able to help others, but each time I felt closer to God's will in my own life.

It was in a Lay Renewal Retreat in Brownwood that I asked the prayers of a small sharing group. I was retired from teaching and had been wanting to write a devotional column for our weekly newspaper, but somehow was reluctant about approaching the editor. I asked them to pray for the Lord's guidance concerning this possibility or opportunity. The next week, I wrote three sample articles and submitted them in person to the editor. He could not have been nicer. Now "Victorious Living," a devotional column, has been published for twenty weeks, and I have not run out of ideas yet.

I am beginning to find the work that God wants me to do. There are many widows in our world today. Many are facing the same difficulties that I faced, and it is impossible for one to fully understand their emotions who has not faced the same experience. I was gratified when my pastor called me to say, "A member of our church has just lost her husband. Maybe you can be of help to her."

One Sunday a widow in my class said to me, "I believe you must pray before you teach. Your lesson met my need today." Oh, yes, I do pray before teaching or speaking that it may be the Lord speaking through me.

I feel closer to the Lord since Lay Renewal. I was not a changed person overnight, but I am growing spiritually and feel God's guidance and presence. I have lost loved ones, faced surgery, and other difficulties, but never doubted that God was with me.

There are possibly many who recognize God in their lives outwardly that do not feel deep within that he should be a part of the thoughts and actions of each day. The witness of others in their spiritual growth can be a powerful force in bringing the kingdom of God to each heart.

V INTERPRETATIONS

1

Renewal—Its Roots and Direction

William Clemmons

THE VINEYARD CONFERENCE CENTER,
LOUISVILLE, KENTUCKY

In all movements, it is difficult to pinpoint an actual starting point—who said or did it first—because movements by their very nature are spontaneous. Many times identical solutions pop up simultaneously at several different places under the direction of many persons at precisely the same time. Those who make things happen all speak to the same generally felt need and, thus, a movement is born.

Because renewal is a movement, it appears very disjointed and unorganized. It offers a great variety of approaches. Each renewal contributor is sure that he/she has invented "the wheel" first and their solution is *the* way.

Though its roots may be found much earlier, renewal arose in the late 1950's and developed throughout the decade of the 1960's. It came about in response to the general religious illness in American Christianity and the nation as a whole. Its message in the 1960's was primarily one of attack against the church and its failure to be "relevant" and "authentic" in the midst of the nation's social upheaval. It was difficult for churches to "press for justice lest they jeopardize the success of revivals, membership drives, building funds, every member canvasses, and the whole life of its institution."

However, there were some persons during those decades who began to ask questions about what the church and Christian life should be. They read books like Bonhoeffer's *Cost of Discipleship*, Trueblood's *The Company of the Committed*, Hoekendijk's *The Church Inside Out*, Edge's *A Quest for Vitality in Religion*, Berton's *The Comfortable Pew*, and Rose's *Who's Killing the Church*. They saw the difference between "What is" and "What could be," and asked the question, "Why not?"

Out of these books there arose a new group of books which began to point the way to solutions: *New Life in the Church* and *Reshaping the Christian Life* by Raines, *The Congregation in Mission* and *God's Colony in Man's World* by Webber, *From Tradition to Mission* by Fisher, *A Call to Commitment* and *Journey Inward; Journey Outward* by O'Conner. Of special interest to Baptists were *The Greening of the church* by Findley Edge, *The Touch of the Spirit* by Ralph Neighbour, *Renew My Church, The Idea of the Laity*, and *Breakthrough into Renewal* by David Haney and *Incendiary Fellowship* by Elton Trueblood. These and other books pointed toward more positive approaches for churches, and in a real sense sounded the tone of hope.

Other writers also indicated new personal and social dimensions of Christianity. These include Thomas Merton, Keith Miller, Bruce Larson, and Lyman Coleman.

Renewal is essentially defined as the work of God in calling his people to new and deeper levels of discipleship. Thomas Merton said that "each individual Christian and each new age of the Church has to make the rediscovery between the outer crust of formality which the Church sometimes acquires from the human natures that compose it and the living inner current of Divine Life." This is the reformation principle of *ecclesia semper riformanda*, or the church always being reformed.

Renewal today is drawing its understandings from six primary streams: (1) the societal upheaval in America in the 1960's; (2) the out-of-datedness of the church in its present institutional forms (which were largely developed between 1740 and 1840); (3) the leftover concerns of the radical wing of the sixteenth-century Reformation which are still alive in the "believers' church" tradition (such as the priesthood of the laity, the concern about economic life-style, the servant posture towards society, the community of faith being a committed covenant people, the cross-denominational, ecumenical fellowship and the exercising of each person's gifts for ministry); (4) the understandings of seventeenth- and eighteenth-century German and English pietism (especially the call to be devotional and meditative people as well as a people on mission); (5) a new interest in biblical and theological studies of what it means to be the people of God; and (6) new understandings from the behavioral sciences about the possibility of personal and corporate change.

In the following summary of thirteen "renewal concerns" can be seen the influence of these six streams:

1. The need to *renew ecclesiastical structures* was one of the earliest cries of the renewal movement as tired, out-of-date structures were no longer able to respond to the new demands being made on the church. New directions were proposed, and this area of renewal continues to occupy much of the concern of many renewalists today. It is interesting that almost every major religious body in America has recently undergone "reorganization."

2. The *recovery of mission* in the life of the church was the heart of renewal. Mission-action has become a byword for many groups in the church. Much of this grew out of a 1961 New Delhi commission on the missionary structures of the church.

3. The basic understanding that the *ministry belongs to the laity* and the concomitant recovery of the equipping ministry as central in the function of the clergy was discussed over and over again in the 1960's. Elton Trueblood in 1952 had said that if the ministry of the ordinary Christian could be recovered in the same manner that the Bible was opened up to the ordinary people four hundred years ago, a new Reformation would take place. Likewise, the study of the Bible passage Ephesians 4:11-12 began a whole new understanding of the role of the pastor as the enabler of the church members for their ministry.

4. A need for *integrity and authenticity concerning social issues* at a time when there seemed to be so much disparity between the gospel's demands and what was going on in the lives of persons,

churches, and denominations focused even more sharply the fact
that ministry was central to the life of the church.

5. Relational theology focused on the need to build *deep and
meaningful relationships* among persons. This was the concern of
the Faith at Work Fellowship and others. Bruce Larson, Ralph
Osborne, and others who were drawn into Faith at Work, began
to develop new understandings about church as a fellowship; a real
community of believers. The renewal of depth relationships was
especially seen in the work of Lyman Coleman (Serendipity books
and workshops) and Keith Miller, who taught us that to be fully
human begins with liking ourselves as the handiwork of God. The
use of the small group, the retreat weekend, relational Bible study,
relational teaching, and the place of self-reflection have all come
as tools of relational theology.

6. Another emphasis has been on the *renewal of the evangelistic
witness* through the Lay Renewal Weekend and Lay Witness Mission.
This strategy uses a lay renewal team which goes into a local church
on a weekend and, through small-group sharing sessions and meetings
at the church, shares its witness. The members tell what they are
experiencing of God's work in their lives. The impact of this form
of evangelistic renewal has already been felt by thousands of churches
of all denominations as lay people form teams and pay their own
way to share with other lay people what God is doing in their lives.
Thus, renewal has been defined for thousands of lay people as a
new experience of a living testimony of Christ's presence in their
lives.

Southern Baptists are emphasizing Renewal Evangelism, a process
of spiritual development called "A Journey into Life-style Evangelism
and Ministry." This is significant in at least two ways. First, it is
an attempt by a major Christian denomination to blend its traditionally strong "journey outward" emphasis of evangelism with the
new breakthrough of the "journey inward" of spiritual renewal.
Secondly, it is an exciting new "maturing process" that ties renewal
and evangelism disciplines and events together, giving continuity
and balance for the church's total journey into evangelism and min-

istry. By tying renewal and evangelism into a journey process, the climate is set for perennial renewal and evangelism.

7. Another definition came primarily through the efforts of the Church of the Saviour in Washington, D. C., where Gordon Cosby and Elizabeth O'Connor have indicated that the renewal starting point is the *deepening of the devotional life.* These two were influenced heavily by Quaker Douglas Steere (and, therefore, by a whole line of Quaker pietists: John Woolman, Rufus Jones, and Thomas Kelly). They, along with Jack Taylor, James Mahoney, and others have given us the combined elements of the search for self through introspection with a new appreciation for Bible study, prayer, and time spent in silence with God. These are combined in what has been called the "critical minimum" for balancing the "journey outward" (a life lived in mission in society) with the "journey inward" (a life lived out of the deep center of relationship with God).

8. Also from the Church of the Saviour have come insights into the *integrity of church membership* where membership in a local church is not taken for granted and requirements for church membership are worked out in a disciplined fellowship. This also was the viewpoint of the book by Findley Edge, *A Quest for Vitality in Religion.*

9. The *charismatic renewal* has affirmed the understanding that all Christians are called to exercise their gifts for ministry within the church and to the world. Churches have come to grips with the Holy Spirit's endowment for service and reconciliation.

10. The renewal of worship, or *liturgical renewal,* began early in the decade of the 1960's. The recovery of celebration in the worship experiences of the church has replaced the often drab and dead formalities of Sunday worship. The use of folk musicals, instruments other than piano and organ, conversation prayer, banners, light shows, the removal of pews, the building of more sanctuaries in the round, the use of lay people as worship leaders, and the formation of worship committees to work with the pastor in building the worship experience on behalf of all of the people—these and

other innovations have given new dimensions to God's worshiping people.

11. The *renewal of the teaching ministry of the church* begins with the understanding that God's people are to be equipped for ministry and witness (Eph. 4:12). It takes seriously two other renewal understandings: (1) that mission is central to the life of the church; and (2) that ministry belongs to the laity. It does not believe that Christian education is an end in itself or is to be used by the church to aggrandize itself (thus making the church a consumer of its own efforts rather than the world a consumer of the church's ministry and witness). Therefore, education is for equipping God's people for mission in the world.

12. The issue of *creative simplicity* in personal and corporate Christian living is being raised with increased vigor today. Persons are becoming more and more aware of the fact that the world does not have an unlimited supply of resources, nor is there an equal distribution of the world's resources so that everyone's basic needs are adequately met. Thus, creative simplicity becomes both an examination of what is enough, as well as how to share with those who do not have basic needs when others have an overabundance of resources.

13. The *role of women in the church* has emerged as one of the pressing issues today. Long overdue, the reevaluation of women's role in the family, in business, and in society in general has caused the church to look again at the biblical and theological statements which affirm that the fellowship of believers is built on "level ground" where there are no distinctions between Greek or Jew, male or female. It has opened up fruitful discussion about women being equally responsible in the church as men (in all positions) and in the discovery of their fulfillment as persons.

Renewal, both personal and corporate, is an ever reoccurring Christian concern—the church always being renewed. From time to time we simply must "pause in a loving study of the church and try to rediscover the lines of its most fervent youth." As the psalmist says, the Lord continually "renews our youth like the eagle's" so that we can once again soar (Ps. 103:5).

2

Reentry

Homer Carter

KIRKWOOD BAPTIST CHURCH,
ST. LOUIS, MISSOURI

One of the most important issues in renewal is reentry. Reentry may sound like some space word and it is. The word also has been adopted to describe the exciting challenge of interrelations between Christians some of whom have been touched by renewal and some who have not. One renewal team member stated that he was really excited when he returned from a Lay Renewal Weekend to his local church. However, the team member did not feel he could say anything about his excitement because many fellow Christians would not understand what he was talking about. Sometimes the church fellowship is thrown out of balance by the enthusiasm of those who participate in renewal and those who do not experience an afterglow. This could be a problem unless appropriate steps are taken. Forewarned is to be forearmed. What can be done about the problem of reentry? This essay seeks to address both laymen and pastors.

The Pastor Is a Key

There are several specific things which the pastor can do to aid in the problem of reentry. First, he should prepare himself for renewal by reading. Someone has suggested that good leadership is finding out the way the people are going and then getting out in front of them. To be in front, the pastor should read twelve or thirteen books on renewal. He who can read and doesn't is worse than he who can't read. Once the pastor is acquainted with the renewal field, he should preach eight to ten sermons on renewal. Suggested topics would include those in this book. Additional topics should include "the eye can't say to the ear I don't need you," "*agape* love," "every Christian a minister," and other solid topics.

Second, the pastor should be aware of possible conflicts of interest. Some in his congregation may favor WIN Evangelism, others renewal evangelism, others revival evangelism, others Bible study evangelism, and others small group evangelism. The pastor should help the people realize that because of the variety of psychological make-up everyone will not respond to all programs equally. God has provided a super-market for his followers. They may pass by and take programs off the shelf which are most helpful to them and leave the others for another time. Reentry can be helped by the supermarket basket concept.

Third, the pastor should affirm both those who are and those who are not touched by renewal. When church members return from a renewal weekend they should have the opportunity to report in the evening service on Sunday or the Wednesday prayer meeting. At the same time the pastor should call on others who have not participated in the renewal journey but who have had a touching experience with Christ where they are.

Fourth, the pastor should teach renewal people the art of being discreet and humble as well as being honest and excited. Serving as the coach-player he should dialogue with the renewal participants constantly.

Fifth, the pastor should not allow himself to be mistakenly threatened by the laity. Unfortunately some pastors want the attention that comes from wearing their many hats of preacher, counselor, administrator, and soul-winner. The pastor should come to the place where he realizes his ministry is that of loosing the laity and letting them go. Finally, the pastor should be as enthusiastic as possible. If the pastor is enthusiastic about renewal most of his congregation most likely will follow his example.

Turned-on People Are Also Keys

The turned-on Christian can do many things to help the problem of reentry. First, he should allow the pastor and the Holy Spirit to instruct him in the art of sharing. Witnessing is sharing with others those things we have both seen and heard from God. Witnessing is not strutting, preening, or boasting. Witnessing abounds in *agape* love that seeks not its own and is secure in the new relationships. Secure persons do not feel compelled to sell or force their experiences on others.

Second, reentry calls for low profiles and an appreciation of the natural glow. The Spirit of God in his people makes them known in his time and way. A patience that waits for apparent changes to be manifested to others can eventually be rewarded by the questions of those who want to be included in on the good news or those who suggest: "Tell me what has happened to you in recent weeks. You're different." It is far more exciting to have someone notice how much more agreeable you are than it is to tell them in advance that you as a changed man intend to be a "more loving person." Wait, and again, let it be stated, wait—wait for the other person to ask you about the change.

Third, be careful about giving a holier-than-thou impression. The history of religious sect groups abounds with accounts of clusters and cloisters of religious folk who received a "special blessing" only to become isolated from their other acquaintances. Many know the "holier-than-thou" syndrome that can encourage a renewed Christian to thank God that he has not made him as those who are unrenewed. This can be done very effectively in coded language if one lacks the courage or awareness to do it directly. Fourth, renewal should build bridges between us and others; it should not erect walls! Renewal frees us to be reconciled. It never creates new estrangements. Renewal gives us new gifts of empathy. It does not place us in the seat of the scornful nor does it stand us in the halls of the judgemental. Renewal surprises us with a new and God-given capacity to affirm some we formerly rejected.

Jesus did not pray for the renewed to be taken from the world of the unrenewed. He prayed for the renewed to keep on being renewed in the midst of darkness. A friend recently returned from a Lay Renewal Weekend with a sense of trauma. She had discovered hordes of lonely people who felt like nobodies in the church. She covenanted to seek out the lonely and alienated in her own congregation. She said, "I am determined to identify with new faces other than my own little group." She regularly sits beside a new face each Sunday in the morning worship hour.

Fifth, returning renewal participants will want to practice the love they learned about during the weekend.

Sixth, renewal participants must guard against a critical spirit toward the pastor. A not unusual myth is to assume that the pastor is not "tuned-in" when in reality he may be very much in touch with the journey. A journeying pastor has often been given the gift of discernment that enables him to help others express renewal experiences and, at the same time, avoid technical jargon that quickly clusters around renewal weekends. Discover, recognize, and utilize the pastor's gift of discernment.

The pastor is the key at the point of responsibility. In most instances he carries the heaviest load of all in administrative accountability. Most churches have learned to give him authority that is equal to his responsibility. Any minister with merit deserves the understanding and support of the pastor.

The pastor is also the communication key. He has opportunities to communicate with more persons than any other person in the congregation. Efforts to work with him in any project can be rewarded with clearer understanding and greater enthusiasm. Not to seek his commitment and understanding is to invite an unwitting lack of communication that could work against any movement in the life of the congregation.

Seventh, when lay team members return home they should beware of the attitude that the only way to accomplish God's work is through renewal and small group techniques. For instance a Sunday School director could try to force the Sunday School members to participate in renewal by the way he structures the opening assembly. A man convinced against his will is of the same opinion still.

Finally, renewal participants should beware of trying to mold every meeting into the pattern of a renewal weekend experience. *Renewal people can become as locked in and stilted in their way of doing things as others.*

Those Not Turned-on Are Keys, Too

After a renewal weekend one church member said, "We had a giant pep rally, but we didn't have any place to go." Another stated, "I didn't get anything out of the renewal weekend. What is everybody talking about?" Another said, "Renewal isn't my thing. I think those so turned-on are just expressing false enthusiasm." It was obvious that these people had missed the blessing of renewal that others had experienced.

What can the not turned-on Christian do to build bridges between themselves and those who have received great joy through renewal? First, be patient. Second, look for things you have in common with those who are talking renewal. Third, invite renewal participants over for a meal and be encouraging. Fourth, go out of the way to show a love for all. Fifth, respect the viewpoints of others and participate in their joy. Sixth, remember there is no requirement that each Christian get excited about renewal evangelism. If you are not turned on by renewal, you need to realize that you are okay. If God has not touched you in the area of renewal, you should not sweat it. You should feel secure in the church work that you are doing. Seventh, deal with feelings of being threatened.

Remember Luke 5? Simon Peter was in the boat with Jesus but everyone does not have to be in the boat to hear the Lord. Those among the crowd on the bank can receive his words in the same way that Peter did while he was in the boat with Christ. God will speak to you who have open ears.

Conclusion

Change is the process by which the future invades our lives, and it inevitably creates anxiety. Our close friends and others will be glad and threatened when they see change in us. No man lives above this anxiety. It is expressed in different ways by different persons. One can expect others to be threatened by any significant change in his being. Even pastors may be threatened by a possible change in the way things have always been done. Remember that conflicts may develop because of change but conflict can be a sign of caring and progress. The gospel does not instruct us to avoid conflict. We are asked to work through the conflict and the threatening relationships until we discover the promised land beyond the wilderness. Those who leave the bondage of Egypt can anticipate the wilderness of confused relationships until the Lord of life has matured us for the crossing of the Jordan.

The closing word is a call to celebration. Celebrate the death, burial, and resurrection of him who makes all renewal a possibility. Celebrate the unity we have in the Christ who honors our uniqueness, the Christ who invites us to discover our uniqueness as we are created in the image of God. Celebrate the Christ who enables us to be free from any need to be conformed into another man's image of what we should be. Celebrate life. He is in all and above all.

3

Journey of a Person

Ras Robinson

CO-DIRECTOR, DIMENSIONS MINISTRIES,
FORT WORTH, TEXAS

Late at night in the hill country of North Georgia I was confronted with:

> And he came to Nazareth. . . . The Spirit of the Lord is upon me, because he hath anointed me to preach the gospel to the poor; he hath sent me to heal the broken-hearted, to preach deliverance to the captives, and recovering of sight to the blind, to set at liberty them that are bruised, to preach the acceptable year of the Lord. . . . This day is this scripture fulfilled in your ears (Luke 4:16-21).

My wife, Beverly, and I were invited to participate that night in an exercise involving the above passage. While attending a conference on renewal evangelism, we were asked to consider the rest of our lives. What was our mission? What would we accomplish? Did being a Christian affect any of these answers? Considering these questions and the circumstances of Jesus launching his public ministry, we were to list the priorities in our lives and share them with each other. We did. Our lists were similar: home, job, church, and ministries with others.

The next morning we were asked to prayerfully consider giving the next two years of our lives as volunteer associates for the Home Mission Board to churches and individuals in the area of renewal evangelism. We would place this assignment in the third place on our list of priorities after home and job—before our own church!

I had problems with this. I had always placed my church after my home and my job. What would the pastor think? What would other church members think? What about the people in the community to whom I sought to give witness of the living Lord? I also had an image of a denominational servant to protect and uphold. Our management (I was working at the Baptist Sunday School Board) stresses, as it should, involvement in our local churches.

God worked marvelously. My pastor and several of my fellow church members became members of my renewal evangelism team. Out of our church came "missionaries" to other churches sharing the realness of Christ in their lives. It was a glorious experience as I became willing to take the risk of exposure and conflict. My journey outward had been properly launched into the deep for the first time.

Walking through our cafeteria during coffee break one morning, I overheard, "Have you read *The Taste of New Wine?*" Someone answered, "Yes, and I have found such delight in *I'm OK, You're OK.*" Seeing the excitement in the eyes of my friends, I began to realize that there was a level of life that I was not experiencing. In my heart I felt left out.

I bought those books and in reading them began to discover a new level of honesty. A certain sense of practicality that suited my life-style. Readers were talking about application of the principles rather than being critical or making comparisons with books in different disciplines. The atmosphere was "alive with living." Something else, the readers seemed mission-oriented: they were doers as well as hearers. They knew why they were doing; they were concerned with motives.

Since it was then part of my assignment to secure and produce Broadman books, I began to search for writers with this new flavor. Much to my disappointment, the well was dry. Even my associates were not sure about my newfound enthusiasm in this area.

Even so, I continued to read. *The Second Touch* and *Habitation of Dragons* were especially helpful (I realize I have now mentioned three Keith Miller books—sorry, but that is the way it was). As our family toured the west in the summer of 1970, Beverly and I read *Habitation of Dragons* aloud to each other. Such honesty and tenderness, such freedom from religious "games"! We would read a while, cry a while, and pray. On those long western highways, alone with our family, God, and the witness of a fine, honest writer, we had a spiritual experience that kicked off much of what we are up to today.

My associates were still suspicious and doubtful but nice. I was hurt, alone, and wanting to fight back. In February, 1971, I told several friends about the joy I was experiencing. Then on a snow-covered Monday a friend called and asked if I would meet Jack Taylor for lunch since he felt we might have some things in common. Jack had flown in from San Antonio to speak to the local pastors' conference luncheon but had no audience. Everyone was snowbound. Over lunch we discussed our similar experiences. He knew something of my joy but more about the source and process of it than I did. I no longer felt on the outside.

After lunch I invited some of my staff to hear Jack share about his journey. We signed him on the spot to write *The Key to Triumphant Living,* a best-seller today. Later we touched base with other good writers and leaders in the renewal movement and have some fine books on the market . . . praise God!

On my way home the day I met Jack Taylor, I said to a friend, "I'm not sure what you fellows are talking about is real but if it is, I want in on it." He invited me over to his house and guided me through the biblical references to the Christ-controlled life, abundant living, and being filled with the Holy Spirit. He talked about confession of sins and claiming God's forgiveness—not just for current sins but those of the past, too. I honestly had never gone back and been specific with God about some of my past. My account with God was out of balance! I was thus introduced to: "If we confess our sins, he is faithful and just to forgive us our sins and to cleanse us from all unrighteousness" (1 John 1:9). I found such release, such peace. I knew God loved me. Now I could look him in the eye. This experience launched me into a new realm: "I am come that they might have life, and that they might have it more abundantly" (John 10:10).

With burdens lifted, I immediately wanted to know all I could about God. His Word became alive for me. I could not read enough. Prayer was now personal and meaningful. God's will for my life came under God's magnifying glass. I began to deal with motives. Was it out of love or duty or oughtness that I did things?

Serving as a renewal evangelism associate with the Home Mission

Board was truly an act of God to call me out into a new level of mission work. It gave me a relationship with my pastor unlike any I had had. He became a close, personal friend. We went to renewal training sessions and to renewal weekends together. He accepted me as a fellow minister! The affirmation felt good. The acceptance from our own church and from other churches of our abilities to work with people felt good. God was in it. People responded. It felt good to do these things at our own expense, on our personal time, with no thought of return. The looks on the faces of those we helped, the letters that came later, and the phone calls were enough.

The journey in my own church was thrilling. We read books, the Bible, and heard tapes on the Christ-controlled life, renewal, and the inner-life. Soon we began to study about spiritual gifts. I was delighted to lead people to begin thinking about their gifts. So many had never even thought of their part in the body of Christ. When they finally began to see, the excitement and joy was wonderful. There were long discussions; changed lives and changed personalities were the results.

We found in our studies and discussions that much chaff had to be eliminated. The wheat remaining was worth sifting. I began to form my own theology about many things, to test it out in the Scriptures, with other writers, and with friends. A new person was growing up inside of me. I began to like and to love him, causing me to like and love others so much better. I could sense the hand of God.

It was through these groups at church that I began to "receive" my own gifts. So many in my church and in other churches were affirming me. My gifts were emerging, growing, and maturing. I had and have spiritual gifts at all three levels of development. Incidentally, one of my problems was that I did not want to fully accept my own gifts. I would rather have the more glamorous ones. Mine seemed rather ordinary. I did not want to just be an "administrator." That sounded too much like what I was trained to do in the secular world. I resisted steadfastly, holding out for prophecy or exhortation.

I can remember the moment when I finally said, "Well, praise God for allowing me to be an administrator. I wonder what he wants me to administer?" There was much to come, now that I had "received" one of my gifts.

There is great variety among God's ministers who are actively engaged in leading persons to him. I noticed that often the persons gifted with great abilities to preach and teach often lacked the abilities to administer. My heart was saddened to learn repeatedly of outstanding preachers, evangelists, and teachers who were rendered ineffective due to lack of good administration. Some good institutions and various religious organizations were experiencing the same fate. Supporting funds from foundations and benevolent friends were of little help except in the short run.

While this knowledge was weighing heavily on my mind, Beverly and I took a few days of vacation in the hill country of west Texas. No telephone, television, or radio. We were cut off from the outside world; even from our children, short of a dire emergency. In this retreat setting there was much time alone with God—time to think again about the rest of our lives. Two years had now elapsed since that beginning in the hills of north Georgia. What has God been saying in these two years? I began to think again about the concept of the body of Christ. My mind was drawn beyond the local church, to the church in the world: God's people everywhere. I began to think of the millions of Christians who live defeated lives, the countless millions who do not know him at all. God had called endless numbers of tremendously gifted preachers, evangelists, and teachers to fulfill his mission to these Christians and non-Christians. Some are effective; many are struggling, some are gone.

On a moonlit night while walking with Beverly in those hills, God began to speak to my heart. He seemed to be saying, "Ras, you remember about those gifts of yours, about the body of Christ concept where the various members need each other? Well, what if you were to make your gifts available to those other ministers of mine who need them? If we think of those as little bonfires, could you not help them to burn brighter? Maybe you could help bring the fires together on occasion and we might have a forest fire!"

We were so excited. Our minds began to sizzle with ideas. We let them run as to how this vision might actualize itself in everyday life. How it might affect our family, my job, our church life? More than any of this was the thought of perhaps leaving the job security I had come to treasure.

The next night in one of those rare moments of nature, we were sitting on top of a hill; the full moon just off the eastern horizon, the setting sun just off the western horizon. A strong wind was blowing through the car. I prayed, Beverly prayed. I resisted the vision, but finally prayed that if God wanted me to go beyond what I was doing, I would be willing to give him my gifts to use in whatever way he saw fit. There was a peace that came with the decision. Somehow the problems did not seem so great.

This happened in the early days of July, 1974. My mind was at ease for several weeks even as we were trying to learn how best to respond to the call and vision. What happened next, during the fall and early winter, was a complete surprise. I knew a little about Satan and his influence but was always afraid to look into it much. Every obstacle in the book was thrown into our path. Church problems, family problems, and interpersonal problems with key friends and associates. It finally came to a head in late November when it seemed that I almost lost it all. Either I must choose to follow the Lord as he had called or it appeared that I would be destroyed. In mid-December, I made the hardest decision of all; I decided in my mind but did not publicly announce that I would end my tenure of fifteen years in my job. Once that was made, the rest was absolutely exciting. I suppose my job had become my idol. God seemed to be saying, "I'll not have that!"

After I made the decision, I came to realize that I had reached already all my boyhood dreams. I had accepted Christ as my personal Savior when I was twelve. God had richly blessed me. I wanted to be of significant service to him. My dreams were also to be a businessman, to write, and to travel. For fifteen years and especially the last six, God had allowed me to bask in the achievement of my goals. Now it was his turn to get some new goals for me. Once I saw this, I knew that I simply could not do the same job for twenty-five more years. I began to wonder why the decision had been so difficult. For any one of my associates could step into my executive job at Broadman, but who could do the unique job God had called me to do?

I was greatly influenced by a church in Alabama where we were holding a lay renewal weekend. The pastor and I hit it off real well together (another gift of mine that allows a special relationship with pastors and leaders). His wife and mine huddled for a while and came up smiling and giggling. Beverly was excited to read a book that the pastor's wife had been teaching with great success in their church—*Fascinating Womanhood* by Helen Andeline. Though the husband is never supposed to read the book, I am told that it has to do with making the husband feel like and be a man through the wife's being in her right relationship with God and her husband. Largely due to her background, Beverly has always been rather independent and strong-willed. This has caused many problems in our marriage since I, too, am a leader.

On Valentine's Day, 1975, Beverly reserved a cabin in a state park nearby, a first for her in this level of initiative. During our time together, she submitted to my leadership and claimed her individuality but in line with God's teaching for the family. I was overcome. Not until then had I fully realized how much a problem in my ministry this had been. This, coupled with the fact that I had been called to preach when I was nineteen, was quite a combination. My mother had always wanted me to preach; I had steadfastly resisted. She had died in the fall of the year! Both these forces hit me. I knew God was speaking, still saying, "I have called you."

I now have two associates, similarly called by God into a special work. God was dealing with three of us simultaneously. We have stepped out on faith, away from security to depend on him to sustain our combined families of twelve. We each have two children. God has led us to commit our gifts to each other and to others as they may need us to lead and organize conferences and seminars and to offer management and marketing consultation and services. We are in the bonfire business and finally the forest fire business for God. It is exciting to see what God will now do.

4

I'm High on Small Groups

William Bangham

LAYMAN, HERITAGE BAPTIST CHURCH,
ANNAPOLIS, MARYLAND

The question is not whether to have small groups within the church or not—we already have them. If that is the question asked—look around. There are Sunday School classes, deacons, WMU circles, this committee and that. People within any church are continually breaking down into small groups for one purpose or another. The real questions are: Why are these groups meeting? (Most groups I have been associated with in the church have been rather dismal affairs—a not uncommon experience.) Are there potentials behind these groups that we are missing? I believe there are. I believe there are solid reasons behind the existence of small groups within the church. I believe that small groups within the church are God-ordained. They are instruments of change: changing our world; changing the institutional church; changing the lives of individuals in them. In short, I am unapologetically high on small groups.

I'm high on them because I'm seeing Christians moving out in small groups from the artificial safety of our sanctuaries and worship halls into a hurting, smoldering world. They are moving out into an arena which daily becomes more polarized between the haves and have-nots. (Lest you wonder which pole the church finds itself gravitating toward, consider the issue raised in our legislatures each year on whether or not to tax the church.) They are meeting the world at the site of its festering sores and oozing wounds in a personal way—face to face—as Jesus did the lepers, the blind men, the captives, along his way—and they are changing it, as he did.

Anyone excluding the social mission of the church from its complexion is as heretical as those who would exclude the spiritual aspect from its depths. When Jesus said to his disciples, "I have set you an example: you are to do as I have done for you" (John 13:16, NEB) he was pointing far beyond the physical symbolism of washing their feet. He was pointing beyond into the world—a world populated with his people—people to whom he was sent to serve, to minister, to redeem—people for whom he was now preparing his disciples that they might also serve, minister, and tell of his redemptive life. Small groups are taking up this discipleship of service and ministry in such diverse ways as the prison-house group that has changed the entire prison system in their state; the group of urban professionals and non-professionals that are bringing modern medicine to residents of a rural area which has had little more than seventeenth-century medical care; a group buying ghetto housing, repairing, renovating, and reselling it to neighborhood residents at cost; and a multitude of other ministries ranging from house groups in trailer courts and apartments, to the young and the elderly, throughout society.

The important aspect of these groups is that they arise from the laity. The small groups do not come down as a program or an emphasis, they arise to a need. Like Jesus, these groups are meeting the world where it hurts. Like him, they are meeting the needs of the world along their journey. As he did, they have recognized that a man with an economic (or other) boot bearing heavily on his throat hears little more than the rattle of his own breath—much less the promise of some far-off salvation—especially when he's not so sure your foot isn't in that boot!

I'm high on small groups because I'm seeing Christians changing the structure of the institutional church through them. Yet change can be frightening—especially where the church is concerned. Part of the responsibility of the church is to hold dear and inviolate those truths entrusted to it—and rightly so. It is not change in the area of truth that excites me—for truth by definition is constant, unyielding and not subject to the winds of change. The emphasis in that first sentence should be on structure—change in structure. We live in a rapidly changing world. My mother learned to read by kerosene lamp, I by incandescent bulb. Who can foresee what will light my children's way? The tempo of change within our society increases each year, and we turn looking more and more for things that are constant, unchanging. Unfortunately we often look for security within structure, while the world whizzes by beyond us. Yet it is not within structure that my security lies—no matter how familiar or comfortable. I am God's son which is a heritage I share with my Lord. Therein lies my security. Jesus has set us an example—we are to wash the feet of the world, though it means change.

Too often our churches are museums or showcases to display our wares. Yet very few come to view them. The majority of our nation will no longer darken the door of a church. They no longer give even lip service to church affiliation. The arena has moved from within the sanctuary (if it was ever really there) to the street, the shop, the middle-class development, the trailer park. Those individuals finding the call of Christ a call to discipleship do not need a museum. They need a fellowship to call forth gifts; to prepare them for ministry; to ordain them for service; to love them when they return from the arena, beaten failures, or rejoice with them in celebration; to reequip them for service and ministry again. They need a warehouse, a well from which they can draw living water.

These needs dictate changes in church structure: Sunday School loses its focus as an evangelistic arm of the church and becomes what it was always meant to be—the educational arm. It becomes a place where new Christians can be nurtured into an ever deepening relationship with their Lord. It becomes a place where the lay ministers of the church are continually being trained and renewed. The deacons cease to be a board of governors and become in-house servants, responsible for the spiritual welfare of the church body. Committees take on new meaning. No longer are they empires within themselves. They become support groups necessary for the ministries ongoing both within and without the physical walls of the church. No longer are ministries contrived, then persons sought to fill them. They arise in response to need. They are nurtured, encouraged, and ordained by the body for as long as that need exists.

The most exciting change is the relationship between the pastor and the laity. Too often the laity view their role as one of support. They will listen mutely to sermons, contribute to some degree monetarily, serve in some capacity as an usher, on a committee, as a teacher—all in support of their pastor. Their unspoken view (but well understood by all) is that their role is to support their pastor, and his is to do the work, the ministry, of the church. How different from Paul's view stated clearly in Ephesians 4:11-12: "And these were his gifts: some to be apostles, some prophets, some evangelists, some pastors and teachers, to equip God's people for work in his service, to the building up of the body of Christ." How exciting to be an equipper of God's people, calling forth their gifts, nurturing them, encouraging them, multiplying the ministry for the building of the body. How exciting to have shepherds moving among us, teaching us, helping us discover what is uniquely us, loving us for what we are, helping us to be all God would have us be.

Finally—and most important—I'm high on small groups because I'm seeing them change lives. Those individuals entering into them are never again quite the same. For some it is a disquieting experience resulting from immaturity, lack of discipline, failure to ever really become a part of the group, insensitivity of the members, bad timing, and a host of other reasons—the chief being the absence of commitment to the leadership of the Holy Spirit. For others, it is a time of blossoming, of taking wing, of excitement and adventure. It is a time of discovering the uniqueness of one's self, of becoming a person of worth, of seeking full participation in the kingdom of God. How does this transpire? It begins by investigating and learning something of the nature of small groups and how people interact within them. It leads through a decision to make a commitment with a group of fellow seekers into a difficult period of growth punctuated with frustration and elation, gradually emerging into a maturing, supportive fellowship which cannot help but overflow from the lives that compose it.

As I pen this, I cannot help but think back over the four years my wife, Dianne, and I have been experientially living within a small group. I remember how we struggled initially—at times staying together only because of our commitment. But gradually, as we prayed together and began to trust one another, sharing more of our lives with each other, something happened. We began to see the potentials lying within each other. We began to accept one another for what we are—and for what we could be.

I realized those individuals loved me in spite of myself. They loved me in spite of my hostility, my pettiness, and the childish things I did. They gave me a vision of my Father's love. If they could love me in spite of my ugliness—how much more could my Father love me. To term that an exciting revelation is meaningless. It was a life-changing revelation! For each of us, in due time, the fellowship of the group met needs as unique as the individuals that compose it. In the inadequacy of our words, in fumbling to minister to one another, the Spirit seemed to transcend our attempts. The living God within each of us filled our relationships with love—and that love overflowed. First it overflowed into the fellowship of our church—relationships there became more important and urgent. Then it overflowed into the arena as each member of the group was lead, one-by-one, into ministries without the walls of the church. The group became a wellspring upon which each could draw for growth, depth, and loving support.

I'm high on small groups because I'm seeing them move Christians into the arena of life where they cannot ignore the needs of mankind. I'm high on small groups because I see them as an ally of the church, an instrument of God bringing his people into a fellowship that demands participation. I'm high on small groups because they're changing lives as a vehicle for finding the abundant life of Christ Jesus. I'm high on small groups because Jesus has set us an example.

Luke tells us that he began his ministry as an itinerant preacher. Then, in verses 12-13, chapter 6, ". . . he went out one day into the hills to pray, and spent the night in prayer to God. When day broke he called his disciples to him, and from among them he chose twelve." Jesus realized that the way was not with the crowd. He realized that once his earthly ministry was over his people would have to minister to one another. So he set us an example of a close, personal fellowship which supports us in our weakness and failure, rejoices with us in celebration—a fellowship which seeks the potentials of our uniqueness through his Spirit. He has set us an example . . . we are and go to do as he has done.